THE
INNOVATION
ECOSYSTEM

MOK O'KEEFFE

R3THINK PRESS

First published in Great Britain 2019
by Rethink Press (www.rethinkpress.com)

Back cover photograph © Arvind Juneja,
Digital University, Poland
Printed and bound by CPI Group (UK) Ltd, Croydon, CR0 4YY

Praise

'Essential reading for any company that wants to get away from innovation being a "eureka" moment to embedding discovery and delivery of ideas into their culture.'
— **Rachel Botsman**
Author, *Who Can You Trust?* and Lecturer, Oxford University

'Mok is pure genius! Not only does he engage the audience from page one, but he takes you on a complete journey. A four-step model to create your own long-term, sustainable Innovation Ecosystem.'
— **Nikki Remmer**
Head of Reputation and Culture, McDonald's UK Ltd

'Innovation can be a daunting word for many business owners; however, *The Innovation Ecosystem* breaks this down into four easy steps. A must-read for businesses on their innovation journey.'
— **Jen Harvey**
Head of Strategy and Operations, Google Launchpad

'A fantastically simple and practical tool to create innovative solutions to complex business issues. It has a brilliant way of simplifying the problem or opportunity and helping create genuinely innovative, exciting solutions.'

— **Claire Hall**
Executive Vice President People,
Menzies Aviation

This book is dedicated to my girls: Olivia, Clara and Allegra.
May you achieve your full potential.
From your loving Uncle

Contents

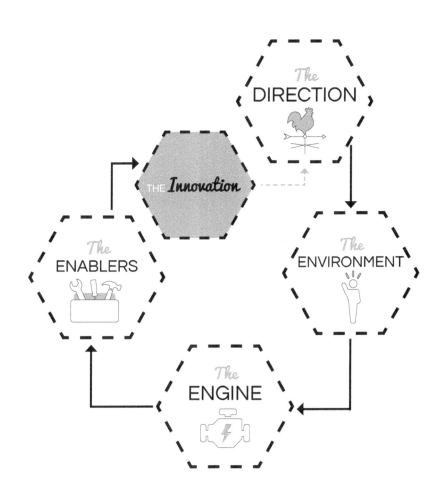

Foreword

'At scale everything breaks.'[1] No matter what you do, keeping things simple and yet scalable is actually the biggest challenge. It's really, really hard. Most things don't work that well at scale, so you need to introduce some complexity, but you have to keep it down.

Urs Hölzle hits the nail right on the head for what seems to go wrong time and again in innovation and digital transformation. Innovation at scale requires complexity – complexity that must be kept simple. It's a formula; an impossible formula, I thought. Until I met Mok.

When I first met him, he was speaking to a roomful of high-street brands, all looking to create sustainable digital transformation whilst struggling to make sense of the noise. His approach was based on a practical, repeatable and proven set of principles, such that I had never seen before; it was a moment of pure happiness/relief for me.

This innovation space is full of highly intelligent people applying years of sectoral knowledge, yet we still find ourselves addressing the same challenges we were facing over a decade ago. Why? Because innovation is complicated at scale, in its infancy, moving at break-neck speed, and there are no mature use cases of success. This makes it messy, and it requires organisations to take a leap of faith that most don't have the appetite for, causing mistakes to be repeated and businesses lost, money squandered, and – in the worst cases – brands dying as a result.

But that day, watching Mok, was the first time I saw the complexity broken down into beautiful logic, with use cases that could be applied across every sector I can think of. 'Preach!' I fan-girled at him, and immediately started reading everything he had written.

When he told me he was writing this book, I rejoiced for us all, and especially all those people who have not yet discovered The Innovation Ecosystem. Mok brilliantly navigates the complexity of scale and sustainability in a crazily fast-moving world of digital revolution; and in this book, he shares with us the ingredients for creating a formula that will work for you or your clients.

If we can all use this knowledge, we will be able to stop circling the drain and take a big step up, so that the next set of challenges we put our minds to in this space can be addressed and resolved quickly. And that is exciting.

— **Emma Mulqueeny OBE**

Introduction

When I first founded The Innovation Beehive ten years ago, I would contact my colleagues in the human resources (HR) community and pitch to them how my new business could help innovation thrive in theirs. This was in 2010, when we were going through the global economic meltdown, and you might think that everyone would have been looking for new and innovative ways to drive growth.

But when speaking to potential clients in HR, I almost always received the same response: that innovation was the responsibility of the marketing team, and HR was responsible for people. Some of the kinder HR folk would offer me up a contact in the marketing function, and I would begin the conversation again.

And the conversation with marketing often didn't go much better. When I spoke about creating a culture of innovation in their business, they would respond that they were the marketing function and responsible for brand and product; culture and people were the responsibility of HR. No one really understood where innovation sat in the organisation. And they certainly were not considering where it intersected with culture.

Over the last ten years, it has been fascinating to see how much this has changed. The Innovation Beehive's clients today include HR Directors, Marketing Directors, Supply Chain Directors, Finance Directors, Managing Directors – the entire breadth of a company is represented in our client base.

And why is that? Because innovation is increasingly being seen (rightly) as vital to everyone's role in the organisation. Innovation is not just about new products, nor is it one pillar of a broader strategy. Innovation is the way you run a business to ensure you stay ahead of the competition and release the potential of your workforce. If you lead a team, a function or a business, innovation is part of your job.

I hope that through the pages of this book you will gain clarity on the four elements you need to turbocharge innovation in your business. Because everyone is responsible for innovation, it is important to have absolute clarity on what innovation actually is. This book will debunk many innovation myths, share examples of how others are innovating, and help you diagnose your own business' innovation opportunity and set yourself up for future success.

You are about to embark on a fantastic journey. Good luck. Keep calm, and keep innovating.

How To Use This Book

Adopt a Parallel-World mindset

This book is based on fifteen years of working with the world's most innovative organisations. It is filled with examples of how to create sustainable innovation in your business. At The Innovation Beehive, we call this 'Stimulus'.

We passionately believe in the power of Stimulus to help you come up with ideas that you would never have created without it. If you look in the same place you have always looked in, or look in the same place as your competition, you will not have new ideas – you will simply have the same ideas as everyone else. Stimulus helps you to see your challenge from a different point of view.

The stories and examples in this book should be treated as Stimulus. I am not suggesting that you simply take what P&G or Ikea have done and implement it into your business or function. Your business has a different customer base, different product, different culture and a whole host of other factors that would make this solution fail. But each story or example will have some principle behind it – two or three intrinsic reasons why the company was able to overcome their challenge.

To use the Stimulus in this book effectively, I will ask you to adopt a 'Parallel-World' mindset – something we teach in our Innovation Capability programmes at The Innovation Beehive. A Parallel-World mindset is one where you take the principles from a piece of Stimulus and then examine your own challenge through the lens of those principles. You ask yourself, 'Knowing that these principles worked successfully in this other business, what new ideas does this spark in me?'

A great example of Parallel-World thinking was practised by the legendary innovator Steve Jobs. When Jobs decided to go into retail, he hired a bunch of senior folk from successful retail brands and challenged them to reinvent computer retailing. Before the Apple stores were opened, buying a computer in store was quite a functional experience, and it was assumed that the customer possessed a fair amount of technical knowledge. This led to unsatisfactory shopping experiences for many people, who had neither the knowledge to know what they needed (or didn't need), nor the confidence to ask.

Apple always prided themselves on creating products that are simple and intuitive. Jobs wanted his new retail stores to deliver the same experience as the products; yet, the prototype stores that the project team initially created and tested with consumers did not fulfil the Apple brand vision. Jobs then used Stimulus and Parallel-World thinking to an extent that can only be described as truly game-changing.

One weekend, whilst waiting for a golf buddy to arrive, Jobs observed the concierge desk at a five-star hotel. He saw guests who had a lack of knowledge, and who did not want to make any mistakes, and employees who skilfully put the customers at ease, guided them through the options, and ensured that they departed the concierge desk confident in the decision they had taken.

Jobs wanted that experience to be replicated in his Apple stores, so he arranged for his retail team to spend time working on the concierge desk in order to understand the Stimulus in greater depth. And once they had done that, they took the principles of what they had experienced and innovated an entirely new concept in IT retail: they invented the iconic Genius

Bar, which turned 'geeks into gods', and made it OK for the customer to ask lots of questions and admit they did not know very much about computers.

By looking at a Parallel World, Apple were able to generate an idea that completely changed the world of IT retail, differentiated them from the competition and has never been successfully replicated by anyone else.

Connecting the dots

Harvard Professor and author of *The Innovator's Dilemma*,[2] Clayton Christensen, says that serial innovators are able to connect the dots.[3] They are able to see patterns in disparate pieces of information. This book connects the dots from organisations as different as McDonald's and GE, Airbnb and Cisco. It identifies key elements that feature in the world's most innovative and successful organisations. A word of warning, though – if you try to implement each of the four elements of The Innovation Ecosystem individually, you will simply end up creating another process or a short-term innovation intervention.

As you read through this book, I invite you to connect the dots between your own businesses and The Innovation Ecosystem. Where have you seen examples of a particular behaviour in your business? Do you already have one of the elements of The

Innovation Ecosystem in place? Reflect upon your own experience of the elements of The Innovation Ecosystem, and use the diagnostic tool to diagnose how they manifest in your organisation.

By considering what you have in your own business – your previous successes and failures – you can use this book to create an Innovation Ecosystem that works in tandem with your unique culture and your customer base, one that will deliver you long-term and sustainable innovation that's aligned to your business objectives and strategy.

Do the work

An innovation *process* is not your end game. The *output* of that innovation process is what's important. This is what we are all trying to achieve – not the process. Sometimes, we need to work with clients to remind them of the fact that innovation is nothing without execution. A great process is just another load of work for your people to do.

I ask you to adopt the same mindset when reading this book. Use it as a template for creating your own Innovation Ecosystem. Work through the exercises at pace, and if you don't know all the answers to each question use your gut feeling to move forward to the next one.

The most important thing is that you use this book as a tool towards execution and implementation. Write all over it, underline words, highlight passages. And above all, compete the exercises – because these will set you on the path towards building an Innovation Ecosystem in your business. If you just read this book and don't fully partake in its content, then you might as well have read the latest Booker Prize winner. You will have passed a pleasant few hours of distraction but someone else will solve the puzzle.

Take time to work through the reflection exercises, and visit our website www.innovationbeehive.com and search for us on YouTube for more information and inspiration. Innovation is as much about how you behave as it is about what you do. Now that you know how to behave whilst reading this book, let's get on and do the work.

CHAPTER ONE

What Is Innovation?

The Innovation Ecosystem and where your opportunity lies

Innovation is everywhere.

If you enter 'innovation' into Google it returns over 1.25 billion search results. Amazon sells over 100,000 books connected to innovation, and the term appears over 4 million times on LinkedIn. Even a casual glance at a broadsheet or a flick through the most recent report from a FTSE-100 company will reveal many appearances of the word 'innovation'. What is innovation?

You might think that because innovation is everywhere there would be a clear understanding of what it is. But in reality, when we first meet with a client we need to work with them to understand what they mean by the term 'innovation' and what it could mean for their business.

I remember a number of years ago, one of the big global consulting houses engaged me to help them to become more innovative. They wanted me to create an intervention for their top 400 fee earners to encourage them to be more innovative. The context of this activity was that they had identified 'innovation' as one of their three strategic pillars. Working with the team, I designed a three-day event with a host of challenges and great Stimulus. They were a tough crowd, but the unanimous feedback was that it was a great event.

It didn't really move the needle forward for them, though. I know that they probably had some stories to share with their clients about how they were working on themselves to become more innovative. They had a few buzz words to use and to weave into pitches and presentations. But as I write this book, many years later, they do not stand out as a particularly innovative organisation.

And the reason, upon reflection, is clear: my client saw innovation as part of a set of strategic objectives and a process which was needed to grow the firm. As a result of this way of seeing innovation, it became an initiative with a series of accompanying tasks.

By contrast, when you spend time with the world's most innovative organisations it quickly becomes clear that innovation is not a strategy or a process:

- Innovation is the fundamental way in which they run their business

- Innovation is their mindset and behaviours

- It is how they work, and not a work process

- It is more than a new product or service offering

- Innovation is in every single part of their business

The opportunity for innovation

Once we have established that innovation should dictate how you run your business, opportunities to innovate appear everywhere. Firstly, it is important to consider where you might innovate. If innovation drives the way you run your business, then innovation can happen in every part of your business – not just with the end user. And it can also happen in every type of business – from an industrial manufacturer of glass to the world's biggest hamburger chain, we have helped every type of business to innovate.

Whilst innovation is often thought of as the invention of new products, we believe that innovation can occur in (at least) four areas.

'Opportunity for innovation' model

Innovation can happen with an organisation's

- Product
- Service
- Experience
- Business processes
- Organisational design

To help you understand where you have an opportunity to innovate, consider the following four questions:

1. Have you identified a solution to a need or problem which your end user is willing to use, if the solution were available?

2. Does your solution align with your brand proposition and your organisational capability?

3. Do you have a channel through which you can distribute your solution to your end user?

4. Could you see a time when the solution will give you sufficient scale or ROI to justify investment?

It does not matter if your innovation is internal or external – the fundamental innovation questions remain the same.

The myth of the lone innovator

We often hear about someone who has toiled away for many years, or had a moment of serendipity or enlightenment, resulting in an innovation that changed everything. But if you look behind these stories, you will find that innovation is not a solo project. We all know that Mark Zuckerberg started Facebook in his dorm at Harvard, but he built a team around him fairly quickly. And Steve Jobs has often been described as the saviour of Apple; but if this were true we would have to disregard the great work done by his Chief Design Officer Sir Jony Ive and thousands of employees, all of whom have contributed to making Apple the world's most valuable brand.[4]

Innovation is a team sport

This fact should be of comfort to corporates. If innovation were restricted to the lone maverick thinker, how could a business continue to innovate? And yet there are many successful organisations continuing to bring new products, services and experiences to market. Others are constantly changing their internal business processes to become faster and better, and to deliver at lower cost.

Innovation requires collaboration, and it relies on structures that encourage this behaviour, if it is going to deliver its full potential. Your people may have many of your best ideas within them. The role of a leader is to release their people's innovation potential and create an Innovation Ecosystem that turns employees into innovators.

The Innovation Ecosystem

Over the last fifteen years, I have been privileged to spend time with some of the world's most innovative and creative organisations. I have met with their leadership, to understand how they create the right conditions for innovation to thrive. And I have also spent time at the front end – with those men and women in innovation teams who are tasked with creating a new product, service, experience or business process.

I have used these experiences to create Stimulus for clients of The Innovation Beehive, and I've helped them to understand how the principles in place at these world-class organisations can be applied to their businesses to solve their particular innovation challenges. I have visited and heard from organisations as varied as GE and WL Gore, from eBay to Google and from Ikea to The Four Seasons. And as I reflected upon how they drive sustainable innovation in their business, a clear pattern began to emerge.

Every time I interacted with a highly innovative organisation, I began to see the same golden thread throughout. It may have been articulated differently in each organisation, but four fundamental elements were always in place. They each had an Innovation Ecosystem.

Each of these businesses had:

- a Direction which focused their people

- an Environment that encouraged experimentation

- an Engine, with structures and processes, that ensured innovation is not overlooked in the relentless need to deliver the day-to-day business

- Enablers, which gave their people the skills, tools and space for innovation to flourish

Does size matter?

Increasingly, we have been looking to the world of start-ups for innovation inspiration. What has become clear is that, even in small start-ups, The Innovation Ecosystem is in place in those businesses that are able to grow and scale quickly. Size does not matter. What matters is having each of the elements embedded in your business.

The four elements of The Innovation Ecosystem – a short overview

The Direction

Most organisations have an articulation of a Vision or a Purpose which expresses why they exist in the world. From this Vision, the Executive Team creates the Business Strategy. The Business Strategy is then translated into Functional objectives before being cascaded down the organisation as individual employee objectives.

Those organisations that are sustainably innovative go one step further. They create a clear Innovation Strategy, which is linked directly to the Business Strategy and then incorporated into the organisation's Purpose. The line of sight from the Innovation Strategy to the Business Strategy is clear, unambiguous and gives a clear Direction.

The Environment

With the publication of Peters and Waterman Jr's seminal work *In Search of Excellence*, business leaders became aware of the impact that culture has on an organisation's performance.[5] Leaders set the tone, and the behaviours that they demonstrate are the ones that get replicated throughout the organisation.

In those organisations that are sustainably innovative, the leadership team members are very deliberate in the way that they encourage experimentation and continually talk about the innovation imperative. The leaders in these businesses create an Environment where collaboration is encouraged. Learning from experimentation is used to make better versions of what has gone before, and their messaging constantly refers to why innovation is important – what I call 'the innovation imperative': what our Innovation Strategy is, and where we will focus.

The Engine

Whilst the first two elements of The Innovation Ecosystem refer to strategic elements, the third element is extremely practical. Within those organisations that are sustainably innovative, there always exists a framework which supports innovation, and which ensures that it is not forgotten in the day-to-day, relentless running of the business.

These businesses put deliberate structures and pro-cesses in place which protect innovation. They also provide mechanisms for ideas to be generated and move through the organisation in order to be iterated, commercialised and implemented.

The Enablers

This final element of The Innovation Ecosystem will Enable you to release the creative potential of your people, but it will have the most impact if done in unison with the other three elements.

This element concerns itself with giving your people the skills, tools and space to Enable them to focus on innovation. Idea-generation techniques can be taught. Innovation processes such as Design Thinking can be studied.

Providing a day of brainstorming training or a mini masterclass in innovation will engage your people, and it may give you a short-term spike; however, beware. The energy created on these days can be a double-edged sword – if you train your people up to be innovative, but don't have an Engine to support them, or your leaders don't encourage them to learn by experimentation, or you don't have a clear sense of your Innovation Direction, you will be wasting your time. At best you will have a small bubble of excite-ment, which will rapidly burst as your people return to their day jobs. At worst you will have shown them a world that could be possible, and then placed it under lock and key. This could result in decreased motivation and engagement.

Inputs and outputs

Innovation is not what you are trying to achieve. I know that sounds odd, since you are reading a book about it. But what I mean by that is that the creation of a fantastic innovation process, with lots of Innovation Ambassadors or companywide hackathons, is not actually your end goal.

Often, we see companies getting so involved in creating an innovation programme that they lose sight of *why* they are focusing on it in the first place. An innovation process is just an Enabler to create the right cultural conditions to deliver a new product, service, experience, organisation or business process.

Your end goal is, in reality, the output of your innovation programme. This is where you deliver on the opportunity for revenue, growth or internal efficiencies. A great innovation programme is just that – a programme. It is not a revenue generator. The four elements of The Innovation Ecosystem are an integrated and balanced system. The four elements are the inputs; and the new product, service, experience, organisation or business process is the output.

Once you have an output, you will need to create a prototype and test it with your end user or stakeholders. The feedback you receive during the Test phase will be used to iterate and improve upon the initial output.

You will then have two options. If the results of the iteration produce an innovation which is likely to achieve your initial target, you will move into the Activation phase. If you have gone through the process of testing and iteration and your innovation is still not fulfilling your end user's needs, you will need to review, and possibly pivot. To do this effectively, you should review your Innovation Ecosystem and consider:

1. Did we set a clear and correct Direction? Was our Innovation Strategy right, and did it align with our Business Strategy?

2. Did we create the right Environment for our people? Did they feel that they had permission to experiment and explore all possible options?

3. Did we have the right Engine in place?

4. Did we follow an innovation process and allow all possible ideas to emerge across the organisation?

5. Did we Enable our people to innovate?

6. Did we give them the right skills and tools to come up with the best ideas?

Ideally, you don't want to get to the Option 2 stage. If you take time now to identify how your organisation performs in each of the four elements of The Innovation Ecosystem, you can put plans in place to ensure a successful outcome. In order to do this, you need to diagnose the current state of play of innovation in your business.

The Innovation Ecosystem Diagnostic

The four elements of The Innovation Ecosystem should be more-or-less in balance if your organisation is to deliver sustainable innovation. If you are able to identify where you sit regarding each element, you will then know where to focus your innovation efforts.

The Innovation Ecosystem Diagnostic tool lets you see how your organisation is performing in each element of The Innovation Ecosystem. It will identify:

1. What element is performing least well and needs immediate attention

2. Where you have strengths on which you can capitalise

Complete The Innovation Ecosystem Diagnostic online at:
https://scorecard.innovationbeehive.co.uk

Once you have completed the diagnostic you will receive a personal report, which will highlight how well your organisation is delivering against each element of The Innovation Ecosystem. You will be able to see where your strengths lie and then consider how you can build upon them; and you will also see your opportunity areas and know where to focus your innovation efforts.

Summary

Any organisation that wants to grow needs to innovate to ensure it is producing services, products, experiences or efficient business processes that remain relevant and useful in the lives of their end users. To build an Ecosystem where innovation is continuous and sustained, business leaders need to articulate a clear Direction for innovation, create the cultural Environment where it is encouraged, put structures and processes in place to protect it from the business-as-usual work, and Enable their people to practise it by giving them the necessary skills, tools and space.

CHAPTER TWO

The Direction: Articulating Your Innovation Strategy

Where are we going?

My favourite book is Lewis Carroll's *Alice in Wonderland*. Whilst reading this to my three nieces as a bedtime story, I was particularly struck by the scene in the woods when Alice meets the Cheshire Cat.

> She went on. 'Would you tell me, please, which way I ought to go from here?'
>
> 'That depends a good deal on where you want to get to,' said the Cat.
>
> 'I don't much care where—' said Alice.

'Then it doesn't matter which way you go,' said the Cat.

'—so long as I get *somewhere*,' Alice added as an explanation.

'Oh, you're sure to do that,' said the Cat, 'if you only walk long enough.'[6]

As it was true for Alice, so it is true for organisations. If you do not know where you are going, you will surely end up somewhere, and it doesn't much matter which way you get there. But those organisations that are sustainably innovative have a clear sense of their Direction of travel. They know where they want to go, and they build the paths (or strategies) that will lead them to their desired destination.

Most organisations have an articulation of their Business Purpose – they are clear on why they exist in the world. The more emotionally compelling Purposes are about more than generating money. They are rallying cries which guide their organisations over time and create alignment. At The Innovation Beehive, we call this 'the duvet chuck' – an inspiring reason for your employees to jump out of bed in the morning and come to work.

This Business Purpose must then be activated. To do this, Executive Teams create their one-, three- and five-year strategies. They should clearly lay out where the organisation will focus its efforts as well as identify the areas where the Executives believe they can win against the competition and deliver the greatest value to their customers and other stakeholders.

To make the Business Strategy a reality, it should then be expressed as Functional objectives; these are then worked into individual objectives for the employees of each function. This process is not earth-shatteringly new, although elements of it are still lacking in many organisations.

As I mentioned when introducing the four Innovation Ecosystem elements, businesses that are sustainably innovative articulate a clear Innovation Strategy, which I call the Innovation Direction. This is linked to, and clearly supports, the delivery of the Business Strategy, with the ultimate intention being to achieve the Business Purpose. And this aligned Direction is articulated in a way that is easily understood by all the employees of the business. It shows them which way to go so that, unlike Alice, they won't just go somewhere but do indeed end up at the best possible journey's end.

Showing the journey –
Facebook's Direction

Mark Zuckerberg created Facebook in his university dorm room in February 2004. Even from its inception, it was about connecting people. At this early stage, it was about connecting a small community at Harvard, which then opened up to other Ivy League institutions before it eventually welcomed the rest of the world.

In 2012, Facebook filed for an Initial Public Offering (IPO). Alongside the preliminary filing, Zuckerberg included an intensely personal letter. In this letter he clearly laid out Facebook's Direction:

> We hope to strengthen how people relate to each other.
>
> Even if our mission sounds big, it starts small – with the relationship between two people.

And he went on to say:

> At Facebook, we build tools to help people connect with the people they want and share what they want, and by doing this we are extending people's capacity to build and maintain relationships.[7]

Zuckerberg was articulating the 'duvet chuck' – he talked about how, right from the very beginning, the Direction of Facebook was to make the world more open and connected. Zuckerberg returns again and again to the idea of why Facebook exists, showing how this guides and explains the company's Innovation Strategy.

F8 is the annual Facebook developers' conference. It is an opportunity for executives from the business to revisit the Direction with the technical folk who will go on to create the code, product and experiences to deliver upon it. Zuckerberg has used this event to clearly lay out Facebook's Business Strategy and share how the Innovation Strategy will help to deliver it. He has built the whole event around Facebook's Direction.

At the 2016 conference, Zuckerberg shared that years one to three were all about creating and delivering Facebook – the platform or ecosystem. In years three to five, innovation focused on product development in three main areas:

- Video
- Search
- Groups

Supporting each of these three innovation opportunities were new products, some developed in-house (Messenger) and some acquired (WhatsApp).

Zuckerberg then shared the Direction for the subsequent five years and highlighted where he wanted teams to focus their future innovation efforts:

- Connectivity

- AI

- VR/AR

Under each of these three strategic platforms he called out potential opportunity areas. But what he excelled at was not limiting the potential for creativity in each of these opportunity areas. He broadly shared how they might be delivered (Connectivity through drones, and AI with language), but he also left blanks – areas to fill in to allow innovation to thrive. He even went as far as to list '????' under VR/AR (virtual reality/augmented reality). Whilst setting a clear Direction for the business, Zuckerberg ensured that there was enough flexibility to respond to future trends, and enough space for people to innovate and release their own creative potential.

Structuring the organisation for innovation – Alphabet

Google is often held up as one of the most innovative organisations in the world. When we talk to executives there, they constantly mention the need to remain agile and nimble as they continue to grow. The growth of Google is well documented; the company moved beyond simply being the world's biggest search engine into areas such as driverless cars, life extension and the video platform YouTube.

As the company expanded, it could have risked losing its focus and its Direction. With so many separate business areas, all housed under Google, it could have become bloated and inefficient. But having a clear sense of Direction is what has kept Google at the number-one spot.

In August 2015, Google was restructured and a new parent company, Alphabet Inc., was formed to 'allow us to keep tremendous focus on the extraordinary opportunities we have inside of Google'.[8] The new Alphabet Inc. has its own CEO, and it is focused on innovating in a specific area. This ensures that the business keeps rigorously to the path it is focused on, without being diverted from its Direction.

Google, now a distinct company within Alphabet, remains the most profitable one of all; the revenue it generates through advertising allows the other Alphabet businesses to operate independently, with their own Directions, safe in the knowledge that the search business is providing the investment funds.

In his blog post, Larry says:

> Alphabet is mostly a collection of companies.
> The largest of which, of course, is Google. This
> newer Google is a bit slimmed down, with
> the companies that are pretty far afield of our
> main Internet products contained in Alphabet
> instead. What do we mean by far afield? Good
> examples are our health efforts: Life Sciences
> (that works on the glucose-sensing contact
> lens), and Calico (focused on longevity).
> Fundamentally, we believe this allows us
> more management scale, as we can run
> things independently that aren't very related.
> Alphabet is about businesses prospering
> through strong leaders and independence.'[9]

The newly formed company has allowed for greater focus in each area in which the business operates, and it has also allowed each unit's CEO to establish a clear sense of Direction.

If you look at Google's IPO letter in 2004, it was very clear that having a focus on the long-term Direction was part of the promise being made to investors:

As a private company, we have concentrated on the long term, and this has served us well. As a public company, we will do the same… If opportunities arise that might cause us to sacrifice short term results but are in the best long term interest of our shareholders, we will take those opportunities. We will have the fortitude to do this. We would request that our shareholders take the long term view… we are trying to look forward as far as we can. Despite the quickly changing business and technology landscape, we try to look at three to five year scenarios in order to decide what to do now… we will not shy away from high-risk, high-reward projects because of short term earnings pressure.[10]

By creating Alphabet, Brin and Page are ensuring that each separate business unit has a razor-sharp Direction. Some businesses, like Google X, are focused on the long-term 'big bets', whilst others, like Google, are focused on more immediate revenue-generating innovations.

Knowing where you can win – Hilton Hotels

Much has been written about the disruptive effect of Airbnb on the hotel industry. Geraldine Calpin,

Hilton Hotels' Chief Marketing Officer, explains how the hotel chain continues to innovate:

> We're not in the lodging industry, but the business of hospitality – people serving people to deliver exceptional experiences... innovation has always been the bedrock of our brand. For example, we were the first hotels with air conditioning and TV's in guest rooms. We may be nearly a century old, but we think like the customers we serve today and we're about delivering exceptional experiences in new ways.[11]

Instead of competing directly with Airbnb, the global hotel group distances itself from the functional need for 'lodgings' and focuses instead on 'hospitality and experience'. This very distinct differentiation has led to a pipeline of innovations such as Digital Key, where guests can see a photo and pre-select their room from a hotel map, order specific refreshments and even open the door from their phone. These innovations sit within the digital world alongside Airbnb, but they deliver differentiated services and experiences.

Hilton also creates innovations on its properties; its Five Feet to Fitness concept responds to a busy traveller's need to keep fit within a hectic schedule by providing a mini-gym in their hotel room. This is not innovating in response to Airbnb's disruption; rather, it is innovating in a space that cannot immediately be occupied by Airbnb but one that satisfies a genuine customer need. This is where Hilton believes it can win.

Communicating to your stakeholders – Adobe and Cisco Systems

Mark Randall is the Chief Strategist and VP of Creativity at Adobe. He has created The Table of Strategic Elements, which lays out the areas of focus for innovation at Adobe.[12]

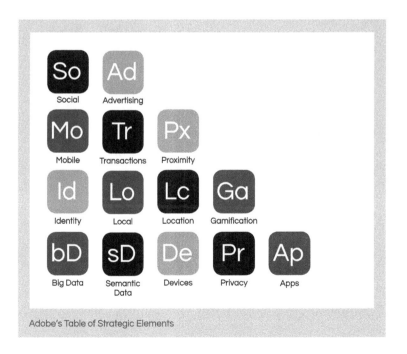

Adobe's Table of Strategic Elements

Randall has created a clear Direction for innovation at Adobe. Each of these elements focuses on a particular strategic area, identified in the business plan as potential growth opportunity areas.

But Randall has gone one step further. Adobe encourages its employees to take single elements from the table and clash them together and generate innovation in the intersection of two different areas. This approach enables the Direction to remain both flexible and focused. What ideas can you have when you combine Identity and Big Data? How could Gamification and Proximity lead you to create new and different products?

The genius of this approach is twofold. Randall has communicated the Direction with a language and a format that speaks very well to the tech engineering and scientific minds of employees at Adobe; but by encouraging experimentation, he has created a methodology which ensures that the innovation conversations taking place within Adobe are unique to them and significantly different from conversations taking place in their competitors' teams.

The exploration of serendipitous connections at Adobe reinvents the Direction each time you come to it, and it ensures that the outcomes of these innovation efforts are products and services that would never be considered by the competition. By creating

The Table of Strategic Elements, Randall has given Adobe a clear sense of Direction. But it is his leadership and the Environment that he has created within Adobe that ensure innovation continues to thrive.

Cisco Systems has used the Stimulus provided by Adobe and created its own Table of Strategic Elements. In the interview at the end of this chapter, you will hear how Cisco uses this to release the creative potential of its workforce. Cisco places its Table of Strategic Elements in the context of an overarching Innovation Strategy.[13]

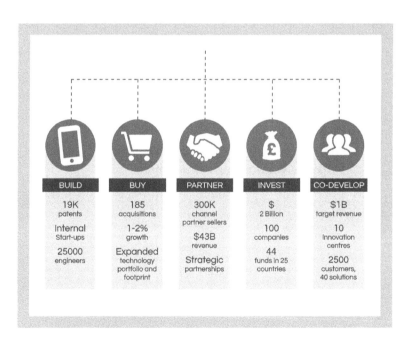

BUILD	BUY	PARTNER	INVEST	CO-DEVELOP
19K patents	185 acquisitions	300K channel partner sellers	$ 2 Billion	$1B target revenue
Internal Start-ups	1-2% growth	$43B revenue	100 companies	10 Innovation centres
25000 engineers	Expanded technology portfolio and footprint	Strategic partnerships	44 funds in 25 countries	2500 customers, 40 solutions

Cisco calls these focus areas 'five pillars to drive strategic growth for the company', and they clearly articulate its Direction,[14] ensuring that it is understood by every employee so that they are able to align each of their innovation efforts under one of the pillars:[15]

- Build: Working within Cisco, with the developer community, or with customers

- Buy: Acquiring or even divestiture, depending on goals

- Partner: Strategically partnering to further build out the business

- Invest: Exploring and seeding investment in specific areas where technology is in its infancy or no dominant technology exists

- Co-develop: Developing new solutions with multi-party teams that include customers, channel partners, start-ups, independent software vendors, and academics

Direction summary

The creation of a Vision, or Purpose, which inspires your employees to throw back the duvet and come to work energised and ready to achieve is an essential building block in a business' success. This Vision, when it is translated into priority and opportunity areas, with goals and targets underneath, is the Business Strategy.

The organisation's Innovation Strategy should be completely aligned to the Business Strategy. It provides new products, services, experiences, organisation design and business improvements, which are able to attract new customers, continue to delight existing ones, and support new and more effective internal processes.

The more clearly you are able to articulate the alignment of the Vision with the Business Strategy, and how it is supported by your Innovation Strategy – your Direction – the more likely it is to be understood by your people, be top of their mind and ensure all three are delivered.

Once you have a Direction, your leaders need to create the culture and Environment that allows it to land and flourish. And this is what we will focus on in the next chapter.

ACTIVITY: ARTICULATING YOUR VISION, BUSINESS STRATEGY AND INNOVATION STRATEGY

Your Vision

Articulate in one sentence why your business exists.

Here are some questions to help you reflect upon why your business exists – what its Purpose is in the world.

1. Go back and review the reasons why the company's founder started the business. Did they have a particular passion? Does this passion manifest itself in some way in the business you have today? Do elements of it still exist, and could you amplify them?

2. What does your business do for your end user? How does it help them to solve a problem, live a better life or achieve other forms of success? If your business didn't exist, what impact would this have on the lives of your customer or end user? How can you articulate the value you bring to their lives?

When thinking about your Purpose, think about how it might be used to motivate your employees to come to work and have a duvet-chuck moment. Your reason for existing must be more than just money. Money is functional and only satisfies in the short term (more of this in Chapter Five).

Your Business Strategy

Many hours are spent developing a Business Strategy, and this will be based on the Executive Team's best guess of where they believe they can win in the market they are operating in.

1. Can you summarise the key focus areas of your Business Strategy?
2. Is your articulation clear and jargon-free?
3. Are you able to communicate clearly how each function contributes to its achievement?

Your Innovation Strategy

1. Have you identified the key areas where innovation can drive growth, value or efficiency?
2. Is there an identifiable link between your innovation 'big bets' and your Business Strategy?
3. Are you innovating in the same place as everyone else? What differentiates you? Why do you believe that you can win in this space?
4. Where else might you focus your innovation effort to ensure you have differentiated ideas?

Now, use the Purpose Architecture on the following page to record and then share your answers.

_____

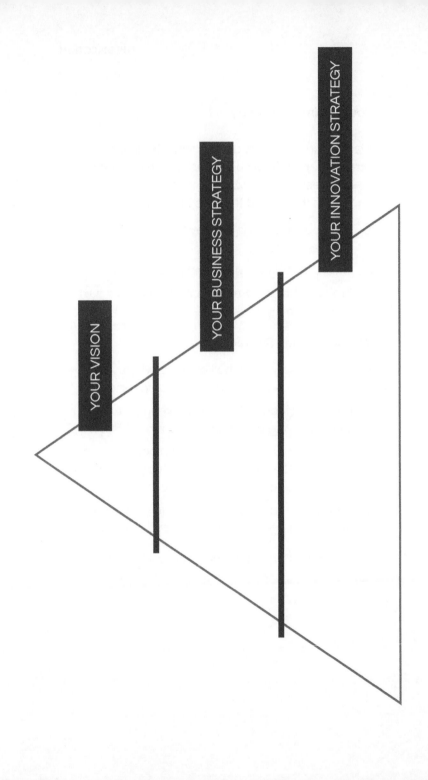

Interview with Harvey Wade, Innovation Lead at Cisco Systems on their Direction

Mok O'Keeffe: *Can you tell us a little bit about your role at Cisco?*

Harvey Wade: My role at Cisco is as an innovation lead. I work in a small team of innovation experts and practitioners; and we work alongside our Cisco leaders and their teams, to really help them to achieve their goals around innovation. That might be around thinking about what they need innovation to do, their Innovation Strategy. It might be around helping to define those ideas, it might be around helping them to implement those ideas, and it might also be around building innovation capability within the organisation. That's a brief overview of what we do; there's obviously a lot more to it than that.

Mok: *Can you give us a definition of what you understand by 'innovation'?*

HW: I think it's really important that who I work with, they are defining what innovation means for them. What do they need innovation to do, what's the job to be done by innovation? And for some people, I think if you look at a lot of the research around innovation you've got sustaining innovation, what do I need to do here and now to make my performance engine work in the best way possible? Make it faster, cheaper, more efficient.

But then you know that the world is changing so you also need to be thinking of the future. What do I need to do in the future, what does my tomorrow world look like and what do I need to do there? And that is more moving into disruptive innovation.

One idea when I think about innovation is, I always work with people and say, well, where are your burning problems, what do you need to think about? And most often I need to encourage people to be thinking about tomorrow, because they are thinking about today, you know, they have all the metrics around today.

So, my definition, to me, around innovation is actually 'problem-solving to create business value', and some of that might be change, some of it might be innovation.

Mok: *In The Innovation Ecosystem, we've identified the first element as being the Direction. I know Cisco's Innovation Direction is around 'Build, Buy, Partner, Invest and Co-develop'. Can you tell us a little more about that and what that might mean?*

HW: Cisco is the first organisation I've worked for that [has] a very clear strategy around innovation.

I think the Build is looking at building internal innovation capability. When you start to move into Buying it. Cisco is well known for the number of acquisitions that it makes and continue[s] to make. And they assimilate it into the business. Some they allow to operate quite separately and some they build in, and we utilise the people and the technology to build better products and services.

Then we do Partnership with the likes of Apple and Ericsson, where we're solving common problems and feel that working together we will have a better outcome.

Then there is Investing. We've got innovation centres around the world, where we bring in start-ups that are working in areas that interest us. We don't take an equity stake, but we will potentially invest, we might buy them, we might partner with them. We really feel that by investing in these organisations they develop the technology and actually Cisco benefits by being on that sort of initial wave of those things.

The final one is Co-develop. An innovation centre in the UK, Idea London, actually is a partnership between EDF, Cisco and University College London. And that really means that we're expanding beyond ourselves.

What's really interesting is, there's some fairly hard metrics in Cisco; it's a very quarterly based company. It's a US company, so it's reporting on a quarterly basis, and in terms of the environment that Cisco tries to create, it tries to allow people to say, 'OK, what you're interested in, you can go and develop.'

One of the things Cisco does, and has done for the last three to four years, is run a global Innovation Challenge – Ideas Anywhere. Cisco has probably around 70,000 to 80,000 employees, and we see around a 50% engagement rate, 40,000 people getting involved. Some people have ideas, but then there's also people joining those teams, collaborating and making them better. There's people actively voting, and people get tokens to invest in the ideas they like best.

Cisco [has] something called Cisco TV, which is a TV system where you can watch all-hands presentations. And they literally will present the top five ideas, and people actually get to see what's been chosen. The most important thing is, they choose three winners, two from the judging panel and one is an employee vote.

But what's more important is, what's really interesting is, the three winning teams get some money personally as a reward. They get money to invest in their idea; but more importantly, they get three months off to work on their idea, which is culturally very counter. People are busy, busy. I think that really helps people to see, OK, if you're doing it at the top, that starts to float down.

I'm working more with leaders to get them to think about that balance between sustaining innovation and disruptive innovation.

What about the future? What will your business look like in two years' time? Leaders need to think about this, you're responsible for your people. You probably ought to spend 10% of your time thinking about that. Also, how are you actually going to resource it? You need to put 10% of resources into that. How do you do that? And so, I'm really helping them to think through those challenges.

I know that being a leader is a very hard role. You've got a lot of things being thrown at you at any one time, from customers, from downwards, from upwards, and I'm trying to work with them to help them to make innovation something that is practical, knowing it's hard work but actually they understand it.

Mok: *One of the things that we've talked about in the past is around the culture that leaders create in the organisation. Why do you think – or how do you think – that the culture at Cisco supports and enables the environment for innovation to thrive?*

HW: I think one of the things that Cisco does, as you probably know, it really sells collaboration technology, so the ability to work from anywhere. Therefore, they have to trust their people that they can work from anywhere; therefore, there's an element of trust that says, 'We've given you a job to do, we will tell you things that you need to do, but we might not tell you how to do those things. We might not tell you where to do those things. If you want to work today out of Starbucks and you think that's a professional way of working, you can demonstrate that, we will be thinking of how you've been affected.'

Most people don't work from Starbucks, by the way, but they do potentially work from home, and there's a trust given to that. And I think that trust then flows through to innovation because you go, 'Well, what do you want to improve, what do you want to do?' And often, the leaders need to do two things. One, they need to encourage those that will naturally be thinking of ideas, but also make almost examples of those people. Say, 'Look, it's OK to test things, to try things.'

Mok: *Tell me about how you deal with failure at Cisco?*

HW: You don't hear people shouting about their failures. But actually, the leaders say, 'We need to talk about this because we don't get everything right.' But we always learn from our failures to do something different.

The example I use is, if you walk along the street and you see a manhole cover off, and you fall down it, and you manage to get back up, would you just walk on or would you stop people who are walking along to say, 'Look, I fell down this, I've just broken my arm.' You'd tell people, it's the natural thing to do.

When we make a mistake, but we've learnt from it, like, walk round the manhole, we need to tell others. It's a responsible thing to do. If you don't tell people what you've done, and it wasn't your fault you fell down there, then it actually builds the whole innovation capability and the organisation's capability to learn and be better.

So, I think we're still getting there, because it's hard to find an environment where you can share those things in a way that will be celebrated and not kind of seen as, 'You made another mistake.'

Mok: *You use the phrase 'innovation capability' there, and the last element of The Innovation Ecosystem is around enabling your people to innovate. Can you tell me a little bit around what you actually do in terms of training and supporting people to give them the tools and the skills and the techniques to innovate?*

HW: What is the problem you're really trying to solve?'

I work with a lot of engineers and, thinking about a problem, they sometimes jump to the first solution.

And so, one of the things that we're trying to build is, 'Really make sure you understand the problem before you try and solve it.' So, we do a lot of workshops where we're really trying to understand, 'Why does the problem exist, who does it impact, who are the people that are being impacted?' Before you move into, 'Let's come up with the solution.'

And what I also find is, Cisco people tend to say, 'We can build it, so let's build it.' And I always come with a counter: Should we build it? Is there a demand for it or is there a desirability for it? And if there is, then great, we've solved that.

So, we do a lot of training in that way. We also are working with leaders to help them to lead for innovation, so helping them to understand, as I mentioned earlier, the Innovation Strategy – what is the job you want innovation to do for you? Leaders may not have the ideas, but they are there to tell their people, 'This is the way that... These are the problems I need to solve. This is the problem that's hurting our business; if we don't solve these problems we may not have a business in the future.'

So, helping leaders to understand their role with innovation, they don't have to come up with all the ideas. How do they get comfortable with not saying 'I don't know'? And the best leaders are the ones that actually can collaborate with their people, and they don't have the answers but they direct people and they make decisions.

Mok: *You've talked about innovation as a function and as a leadership competence. It's an eternal debate, but who do you think owns innovation in an organisation?*

HW: That's a really interesting question because, for me, the leaders are responsible for the Direction. They need to understand the problems that they would like to be solved. So, I think it's really important that they own and are responsible for it, they're visibly active in it.

But in terms of the overall ownership, it has to be every individual has a responsibility, and what often happens in an organisation is that people who come up with the ideas are celebrated. There's often people sitting in a group that don't have ideas, but they make the idea better. Or, 'I connected this person with Mary over there; that made the idea even better, I've then helped to implement the idea.' Because that's really hard as well. 'I've then told everybody about the idea because it's got to be a team effort.'

And so, for me it's a mixture of a strategic direction coming from leaders but also then being aware of the cultural environment to engage people in this, and to engage people I need to help them to understand what's in it for those guys – I need to answer that question.

So, I think the ownership lies with everybody.

Mok: *What do you think are the barriers to creating The Innovation Ecosystem in an organisation?*

HW: The main barriers normally lie around: you can have a great strategy, but if you don't think about the culture and how to engage people it just won't happen. I've seen a lot of things where, actually, people don't feel in a safe environment. Innovation is risky. Why would I do something I'm very safe with, doing my job, and suggest something that's a little bit out there if I feel that it's an unsafe environment?

So, how do we make people feel safe? You've almost got to take care of people from a safety and hygiene perspective. Nobody's going to give you a great idea on the next big thing if, for example, their chair is broken and for the last three weeks you have not fixed it and they've been telling you for three weeks it's not been fixed. So, you have to take care of people.

For me, innovation culture is a very precious thing. It's a little bit like reputation. You build a reputation, do one thing and you've lost your reputation, and there's lots of examples. Innovation culture or engagement, engage, engage, engage and then something happens, and they go, 'Why have you done that?'

Mok: *How do you measure innovation? Do we need to think about the metrics differently?*

HW: Yes. I think metrics are often thought about last, and they're normally crassly thought about, and I always like to think about, what's the outcome that you want to have? And you can normally measure that by a number of ideas and how many ideas we get implemented and how much revenue... That's basic stuff.

What I think is more interesting is, how do you measure the effectiveness of your innovation, how do you measure culture? People think about, 'Let's do a survey.' I don't know how many surveys you get but it kind of... You get either the most engaged people completing a survey, but actually you don't get a lot of people who you really want to complete a survey, and then you get also the people with a big axe to grind will complete the survey. So, you get the two extremes, which we kind of see all around elections. The silent majority is not heard.

So, I always like to think about bringing in an element of, 'If this is successful, what will you be doing differently, what will you be seeing and hearing that is different, how will it feel different, what will you see from people?' And it's trying to get people into that future state. And then set KPIs from there.

CHAPTER THREE

The Environment

Leaders who encourage, enable and reward innovation

A clear sense of Direction ensures that your people know the road of travel. This is the first element of The Innovation Ecosystem. However, it is not enough to set a Direction and assume that everyone will know how to move forward.

The key to ensuring that your Innovation Direction is activated lies in the leadership of your organisation. As well as setting the Direction, leaders must encourage employees to keep moving forward and reward them for each milestone of the journey. The organisation's culture and its leadership can either make innovation a priority in employees' minds, or they can actively contribute to an Environment where innovation is viewed with a feeling of disengaged cynicism.

The latter is the death knell of innovation. Disengaged cynicism is found in organisations where innovation is talked about in strategy days, appears in competency frameworks and may even be written on the walls of reception, but where individuals and teams are measured on short-term, 'business-as-usual' decision making. Coupled with this, we may observe a leadership team which fails to reward experimentation or foster the Environment where it feels OK to experiment, learn or even fail.

Soren Kaplan summarised this well in an article for the *Harvard Business Review*:

> Employees have experiences that come from a leader's conscious and unconscious decisions and behaviours. Those experiences shape assumptions about what behaviour is desirable or undesirable.[16]

She argues that a leader's actions shape employees' behaviour. 'Innovation' is a much-favoured word of leadership but, as the old adage goes, *actions speak far louder than words.*

A few years ago, I was privileged enough to spend time with a leadership team at Ikea. These leaders shared the concept of a 'values and leadership bubble'. They likened the role of leadership to holding a fragile bubble – the kind that you might see a child blowing at a birthday party.

The team members shared that Ikea leaders are holding the values and behaviours of the organisation in their hands, like a bubble. And just like a bubble, once it is burst it can never be put back together again. This responsibility led them to be very conscious about their own behaviours, their use of language and the message this conveyed to the wider organisation.

The Chief Innovation Officer

I have noticed a new role emerging in businesses over the last few years – the Chief Innovation Officer. In some organisations this is given a different title, but in all instances there is a 'person' who is responsible for innovation.

I understand the increased popularity and convenience of having a singular focus point for innovation – the board wants to send out a clear signal that they mean business around innovation. The new role is intended to keep innovation on the agenda and ensure that employees are not only focusing on business-as-usual.

However, over the years, my team and I have experienced varying successes with this designated innovation leader. Dedicated innovation roles and teams can be successful when they:

1. Put the right measures in place for innovation

2. Work with HR to build the right organisational structure

3. Actively seek out external partners and suppliers to bring in fresh thinking

4. Work with the Learning function to support efforts to develop innovation skills and the sharing of best practice

5. Look for new market spaces to grow

I call these The CIO's Five Conditions of Success.

By contrast, sometimes the introduction of an innovation role can be detrimental to innovation. At its very extreme, having a dedicated leader for innovation can mean that they are given the responsibility to 'own innovation', and an established norm can be created where all innovation goes through them or their team – and if it doesn't go through them, it is not 'innovation'. This results in innovations being slowed down as permission is sought from the innovation team to innovate.

We have also observed subconscious messaging, after the introduction of the CIO role, which implies that innovation is now being taken care of elsewhere in the organisation, and no one in any other function has to concern themselves with it. Finally, we have seen examples where innovation teams seek to 'own' innovations created elsewhere in the organisation, in which they had no involvement. This can lead to a strained working environment and one team taking the credit and being rewarded for another team's work.

Crucially, in order to achieve any of The CIO's Five Conditions of Success listed above, the CIO must have a realistic budget. Without finance and the ability to direct seed funding to nascent ideas, an innovation leader will have little impact or real ability to make change happen. At worst they will be reduced to walking around the organisation with a bunch of post-it notes facilitating brainstorms or creating colourful open-plan offices in the hope of encouraging creativity and innovation.

What they won't be able to do is light the fire of creativity across the organisation, build a depth of innovation skill, or identify and exploit new growth areas. If you can't give your innovation lead a budget, then you should consider not appointing them at all. Instead, look on YouTube and send your employees a few links. It will achieve about the same value, and at least you will save on head count.

Iconic Actions

In those businesses where innovation is turbocharged, it is encouraged and enabled by the leadership team. We have observed these teams delivering 'Iconic Actions' to inspire their workforce. These actions bring the Direction to life in the day-to-day environment and ensure that innovation stays top of mind.

Zipcar created a spectacular Iconic Action. When the founders created their business in 2000, it disrupted the model of car rental and heralded the beginning of 'the sharing economy'.[17] However, the entire customer experience was designed for use on a desktop or laptop, and – in a world that was rapidly transitioning to mobile as a priority – this proved a significant cause for concern.

Zipcar realised that it needed to move swiftly to a mobile platform, but, with a business that was so entrenched in the old ways of delivering the customer proposition on laptop and desktop, the company decided that it had to do something radical to communicate that need for change. Company leaders invited employees to a meeting where they explained the mobile imperative and the need for innovation on the new mobile platform. They clearly communicated the Direction.

And then they did something to really bring the innovation imperative to life and create the right Environment: they handed out sledgehammers and invited employees to smash up a desktop computer. This iconic leadership action spoke far louder about the compelling need for change and new Innovation Strategy than any PowerPoint deck or CEO speech ever could.

Organise to innovate

The role that leaders play in encouraging innovation is evident at WL Gore, which is led by inspirational CEO Terri Kelly. Kelly believes passionately that the continued success of 'the enterprise' will be down to the way people are led.

At Gore, leadership is not an attribute of a particular job role or an individual's position in the organisation. Instead, it operates with the concept of 'emergent leadership' and insists employees can only be leaders if others are prepared to follow them. This is an essential part of their 'lattice structure' where hierarchy is replaced by connectivity – 'leaders emerge', and leadership is not inherent in a job title or status. 'Associates' cluster around innovation opportunities which they are passionate about, and there is a significant amount of internal selling to encourage colleagues to support or to join a particular team's innovation efforts.

This connectivity is promoted by offices with no more than 250 employees. Kelly admits that other CEOs 'look at this (as an) unbelievable expense, but we see it as a catalyst for growth'.[18] This focus on the power of small teams has been taken a stage further by Jeff Bezos at Amazon, who has implemented a 'two pizza rule'.[19] He insists that no meeting at Amazon should have more people attending than can be fed by two pizzas. This, he claims, improves productivity, ensures everyone's point of view is heard and promotes the Environment of collaboration, with people connecting on a very human and authentic level.

Tony Hsieh, the unconventional and enigmatic CEO of online retailer Zappos, has transitioned the business to a 'holocracy',[20] where there are no bosses or direct reports. Instead, there are 'lead links' who oversee 'circles' of work. Hsieh believes that by breaking down hierarchy, employees who are traditionally viewed as 'lower level' are instead encouraged to have a greater impact and to contribute more. As they are often in direct contact with the customer, the employees' experiences and the insights they bring can ensure that Zappos continues to operate in an environment of rapid innovation. Hsieh argues that this approach will ensure that Zappos does not lose its agility, productivity or culture as it continues to grow. He explained:

> As companies get bigger, they become slower moving; there's more bureaucracy. And I don't think any manager is purposely thinking 'how can I become more bureaucratic?'[21]

Hsieh has deliberately created an Environment where connectivity is the norm.

The importance of language

The Chinese white-goods manufacturer Haier uses language as an Iconic Action. Haier doesn't have 'employees' but instead has 'makers'. Its philosophy is that it is everyone's job to make things, not to attend meetings or clear their email inbox. Disney calls its employees 'imagineers' – a clear message to think creatively and differently. WL Gore uses language in a similar way, where 'expenses' are renamed 'investments'. These three organisations use language which is output-focused – investing to make innovations, rather than spending money, and being a maker or imagineer, rather than pigeonholed into the role of an employee who has a set number of tasks to complete.

Encourage experimentation

To create the Environment for innovation, leaders must examine how their language and behaviours promote or detract from experimentation and calculated risk taking. Facebook, in its early days, had the famous mantra: 'Move fast and break things'. And, for a time, this worked very well for them.

The 'Move fast' philosophy encouraged the development of new innovations, which often went live before they were 100% functional. But, by placing innovations in front of customers before they were fully ready, employees would have to spend time fixing a number of bugs which emerged once the Facebook community started to engage with the new innovation. Rather than promoting speed, it actually slowed Facebook, and its engineering partners, down.

In 2014, Zuckerberg announced that the mantra would change to the less catchy 'Move fast, with stable infrastructure'. This was a sign of a new maturity at Facebook and an acceptance that the behaviours that had driven its success to date were not the behaviours that would sustain it. The shift was subtle – speed is still an essential part of their culture, and the new mantra was not contradicting the message that growth would still come from exciting innovations – but these new innovations would be launched right first time.

Rapid iteration is still at the core of Facebook's approach to innovation, but there is no longer an acceptance that iteration should be done in public view: 'Because when you build something that you don't have to fix ten times, you can move forward on top of what you've built,' says Zuckerberg. 'These are real changes that we're making so people can rely on us as a critical infrastructure for building all of their apps across every mobile platform.'[22]

Experimentation is still at the core of how Facebook operates, and at any one time there can be multiple versions of the platform running internally. This allows engineers to rapidly prototype iterations and see how they impact on the metrics that Facebook holds to be important, as Zuckerberg explains:

> I want to empower people at the company
> to try things out… what it leads us to do is
> build a ton of infrastructure that empowers
> engineers to try a lot of stuff… there are
> thousands of different versions of Facebook
> running, and any engineer is empowered to
> try something out and they get this report of
> how it performs on all of the metrics we care
> about… sharing, time spent, engagement,
> amount of friends that people have and the
> amount of money we make…[23]

Reward learning

Experimentation must be at the core of any Environment of innovation, with leaders actively celebrating those in their business who have tried to push the innovation envelope. And once your people have experimented, you need to reward them in order to encourage them and others to do it again and again.

Tata Group's Innovation Forum introduced an award programme called Innovista. Awards for the competition focus on three categories:

1. Promising Innovations: those that have been successfully implemented

2. The Leading Edge: those that are in the idea stage

3. Dare to Try: those that teach us what doesn't work

The Dare to Try Award was won by teams who made unsuccessful, but ambitious, attempts to innovate. It recognised that, even when innovations don't quite work, there are lessons to be learnt. By rewarding a culture of continual experimentation, innovation efforts at Tata are more likely to be repeated and become part of the Environment.

Sunil Sinha, an executive at Tata, explains why Dare to Try was so crucial in creating the Environment where innovation would thrive and, at the same time, supporting a culture of learning:

> Too much of our culture was about good news. Our meetings were designed to talk about the good news. Now the whole paradigm is changing. People are passionately telling us what has failed and more importantly, what they have learned about why it failed.[24]

Examples of award winners include a new type of car door made from plastic – which fell short of safety requirements – and a water purification and filtration system which initially failed but eventually became Tata Swatch and sold 1.5 million units in its first year of launch.[25]

Jeff Bezos described the intersection of experimentation, innovation and learning when he talked about watching a toddler playing with a cognitive development game. The child had to put a circle in a circle hole, a star in a star hole, etc. At first, the toddler got it wrong and failed to put the right shape in the corresponding hole. Bezos explained that, rather than be embarrassed, the child kept trying and eventually got it right:

> At Amazon, we have to grow the size of our
> failures as the size of our company grows…
> we have to make bigger and bigger failures
> – otherwise none of our failures will be
> needle movers… failure and invention are
> inseparable twins.[26]

Break down the silos

Monzo is an online challenger bank which has distinguished itself by getting millennials interested in banking. It has been referred to as 'the Facebook of banking'.[27]

I had the pleasure of hearing Monzo's CEO, Tom Blomfield, speak at the Cass Business School in London. Monzo's employee numbers had grown from sixty to 300 in a year, and I asked him what impact this had on his leadership style and whether he has seen an evolution in his style as the company has grown. He replied:

> It's hard. At first, I thought it would be exactly
> the same, but from sixty to 300 people, stuff
> slowed down and we didn't iterate quickly
> enough. Your role as a leader is to encourage
> people to keep experimenting and being
> innovative.

He was describing the Environment perfectly.

He shared a story of meeting a Monzo employee, 'over a burger', and hearing their frustration at not being able to move forward with their latest idea. He couldn't get it through legal, marketing and brand, and his great idea was grinding to a halt. Tom promised to help him cut through the red tape and break down the silos. He wanted to role model his leadership message that at Monzo 'you can build it'.

With Tom's support, the employee's idea was launched. It's called Coin Jar: whenever a customer makes a purchase of over a pound using a Monzo card, the Coin Jar rounds up the purchase to the nearest pound and automatically deposits the extra pence into a savings account. This Coin Jar account encourages customers who think they don't have enough money to save to make micro savings, and, 'According to the old cliché, a little goes a long way. And we think that's especially true when you're saving. By putting small amounts of money aside on a regular basis, over time you'll see your savings grow.'[28]

Tom's iconic act of leadership helped to launch a great new product by breaking down silos at Monzo and also ensured his employee remained engaged and encouraged to continue innovating. His leadership sent out a clear message about the kind of Environment he wanted to create at Monzo, one where innovation and creativity are encouraged and rewarded.

Message the innovation imperative

Senior leaders actively referring to 'the innovation imperative' is vital if it is to become a priority for the workforce. David Fairhurst, Executive Vice President and Chief People Officer for McDonald's, talks about a major cultural shift required in the restaurant chain if it is to meet and exceed the increasing expectation of its customers: 'The speed and pace of change, and customer expectation is continuing to evolve and it is a bit like being on an escalator,' he said. 'And it's getting faster and faster. Yesterday's "outstanding" for a customer, for a product or service is today's "normal".'[29]

Fairhurst is being very explicit about the need for innovation. He goes on to explain that one of the ways in which McDonald's can deliver its ambitious growth plans and continue to serve more than 68 million customers a day is through creating the right culture in the business. Leaders must encourage experimentation and a workplace where it is OK to experiment – and take learnings back into the business.

Environment summary

An Environment for innovation is one where employees are connected and share knowledge across the business. Leaders must find a way to encourage connectivity, even if it impacts on traditional command and control structures. Whilst there may be initial fear about a loss of status, everyone will share in a future that is built upon a strong innovation pipeline.

Finally, and most crucially, leaders must continue to talk about the innovation imperative. It is not enough to simply mention it in the annual report, at the annual conference and at one all-hands meeting. All leaders must explain and then continue to talk about the innovation Direction. When the innovation imperative is re-enforced in team meetings, one-to-ones, performance reviews and at as many other opportunities as possible, then the organisation will understand that innovation is part of everyone's job and that it is vital for shared future success.

ACTIVITY: CREATING YOUR ENVIRONMENT PILLAR

To help you create your Environment pillar, consider the following questions:

1. How have you dealt with failure – either your own or that of a team member?

2. When was the last time you talked to a colleague about the innovation imperative? How did you describe the Direction to ensure that they understood their role in delivering it?

3. Reflect upon the last time a colleague suggested a new way of doing things. How did you respond?

4. How could you work – and encourage your teams to work – cross-functionally?

5. What Iconic Actions have you or your leadership team undertaken to encourage innovation?

6. How have you signalled that innovation is everyone's job?

Interview with Nic Roome, Head of Ground Control, Airbnb London

Mok: *Thank you so much for spending some time with us today to [help us] understand a little bit about the environment and the culture at Airbnb. So, before we launch into that, can you just tell us a little bit about your career history and how you arrived at Airbnb?*

NR: Somebody said, 'Why don't you rent your room on Airbnb?' This is going to sound so cheesy. So, I rented my room on Airbnb and started to build up my income.

As part of that, I got invited to the Airbnb offices on a fairly regular basis as a sort of host/business collaboration of how we are doing, what's working for you as a host, what's not working for you as a host, and talking to the local community. And from that point I just thought, these guys are really, really lovely, and I just asked for a job. Hence, I had no idea what was going to be in store, and I found myself six years on here at Airbnb.

Mok: *Wow! I mean, I've actually been to one of your sort of host events as well, you really do build quite close connections with your hosts, don't you, and listen to them and bring them into the building and get their point of view?*

NR: Absolutely, yes, we have a dedicated team here; we bring hosts in so that we can engage with them and listen to their stories, their fascinating stories. Often, they've led team meetings whereby we've had six or seven hosts kind of share their whys and wherefores around hosting, their best tips and practices, which often leads to life advice, which when you boil it down is good because hosting is a personal thing, so you see a lot of personality come out.

Mok: *Six years in, you are Head of Ground Control. Tell us a little bit about what that means and also, from Airbnb, what is Ground Control?*

NR: Head of Ground Control is quite a highfalutin title. Ground Control Manager. But I don't want to kind of overplay that, we're always very humble and actually, interestingly enough, not many people with our email signatures do put the level at which they work. So, you'll simply work in 'finance' or 'talent' or 'IT'. It's actually quite an interesting kind of concept.

Going back to your question...

Mok: *What is Ground Control and what's your role within that?*

NR: Ground Control means a few different things depending on the size of the office that we're in. We are part of the umbrella of employee experience, so in London that means we partner with various different teams such as facilities and food and recruitment and our learning and development teams to make sure that the employee experience on a day-to-day level is channelled through ourselves and given back to the team in a sort of seamless and natural manner.

We bring the team together over different communication strategies, over team meetings, over cultural moments, how we feed each other, how we interact and learn and sort of play together. If you want it distilled down into being the sort of most consummate host possible for the office.

Mok: *And so, you talked there about the employee experience, or we call it Employee Value Proposition. What is the employee experience at Airbnb that you're curating and creating?*

NR: Employee experience essentially starts from the very second we engage with a person, whether that's reaching out to a candidate or a candidate comes to us, it starts from that very moment. So, it's the whole experience from end to end, to the day that their journey with us ends. It's all of those daily interactions, it's all of the meaningful moments and it's all of the communication that they have and development that they have within their role. We are there to support them in each of those steps.

Mok: *So, you have quite a unique culture at Airbnb; do you want to share a little bit around what the culture is, your* *values, and then how that actually manifests itself for the employees?*

NR: We're always looking and we're always asking the question of ourselves, 'What is culture and what does it mean to us?' So, if you wind back to when it was just the three founders, then it was just three guys in an apartment pushing themselves to the limit to make this product happen. If you wind forward ten years, we find ourselves with thousands of employees across multiple countries with millions of listings and millions of nights booked, and how do we contain that?

I guess culture can never be contained. It's always an evolution and you have to kind of be open to the ever-changing parameters and the idea that it's not set in stone. However, having said that, there are a few things that you can always come back to.

I think one of the things that we've all found, and you can apply this to pretty much any culture, is the fact that you have shared assumptions. So, when you walk into the office, I have a shared assumption that this person feels like me, acts like me, I understand them, I have immediate empathy for that person – pretty much the shared assumption is, if this situation occurs, I know that we'll all react in the same manner. Or, we've all got each other's back. Pretty much you have a shared assumption when you go to a certain restaurant that you understand that the people in that restaurant will be expecting the same service from that chef or from that plate of food that's put in front of them.

Mok: *Consistent behaviour or consistent promise?*

NR: Exactly. Yes, exactly, it's the shared belief that you have together, and I have a really great quote – 'The culture of a group can be defined as a pattern of shared basic assumptions, learned by a group as it solves its problems of external adaption and internal integration' [Edgar H Schein].

It's understanding that we can learn and organise ourselves together over one goal and one mission. How does that come out, how does that come into play on a day-to-day basis? It's like visible and invisible manifestations of culture. So, the invisible is how we're going to behave and relate and decide together. And the visible ones can be more, what we call like a declared difference. So, it's, 'This is us, this is Airbnb, this is who we are, what we stand for.' It's almost like our line in the sand, if you want. It's what sets us apart from the rest of the world.

So that's easy to identify. We also have a strong leadership, so we're lucky to still have our three founders within a growing company, which is kind of a rarity nowadays. And we're lucky to have those founders present and also the executive staff that have been in tenure for a very long time; they show up, they are the living, breathing embodiment of these cultures, and by those mastheads taking forward our beliefs and our strategies and our core values, then therefore that will have a great trickle-down effect internally.

And also, our physical space as well, this is where you have certain manifestations of our culture. So, we're sitting in a room that's been inspired by a listing in Japan, and it sort of has little bamboo on the wall, it's very simple and minimalistic but we have this around our global offices where our culture is basically a manifestation of our product, which is essentially people's homes and any other kind of lodging that they wish to share. We bring that internally so that we live through our product, which again is a great contributor.

And it constantly reminds you that this is what you're about. You know, we are effectively sitting in a representation of someone's home in Japan that they're making some spare money on, and it kind of links us back to that host, to whoever she or he is... we have four core values within Airbnb.

So, in the inspirational, top of the list for me is, 'Be a host'. So, this is somebody who cares for others and makes them feel like they belong. Encourage others to participate to their fullest, and listen and communicate openly, and set those clear expectations.

So, in essence, you're trying to anticipate everyone else's needs around you. 'Championing the mission' is basically, we do work that, our mission is to create a world where anyone can belong anywhere, and we prioritise any work that advances that mission and impacts the community in a positive way, and build with the long term in mind – so it's not just a sort of quick win.

Also, we have a value called 'Embrace the adventure'. It's actually the adventure of curiosity, it's your own journey. So, it's like, be curious and ask for help. It's, how can you demonstrate an ability to grow and own and learn from your mistakes, and bringing your joy and optimism to work as well? So, it's that sort of, almost adventure of your own progress and your own self, learning – a mental journey, if you like.

Mok: *Curiosity is a vital part of innovation. Being curious about the world. We've seen it time and time again; Clayton Christensen points out that curiosity is a key element for innovators.*

You talked to me earlier on about being a serial entrepreneur and being scrappy as a philosophy or approach at Airbnb. Tell us a little bit more about that and what it means to you.

NR: Absolutely. So, 'Being a cereal entrepreneur' is the fourth core value. It's about applying bold and original thinking to any project or situation that you come across. You've got to imagine the ideal outcome and then be resourceful to make the outcome a reality. So, being resourceful in simple terms is being scrappy and just getting the job done.

It was born – just as a little caveat, a historical cultural reference – from our founders during the Obama/McCain campaign in 2008. The founders were down on their heels, they had very little money, they were maxing out their credit cards and – this is all online if anybody wants to go back and verify – they created two cereal boxes, Obama Os and Captain McCains. They did these great cartoon-character drawings on the cover, stuffed them with actual real cereals that they bought from a supermarket, and then sold them for – I think it was $40 each, and made enough money to cover the debts that they'd accrued.

Mok: *That's fantastic. That's innovation and action, isn't it?*

NR: Absolutely, hence why it's a 'cereal' entrepreneur, spelt like 'breakfast cereal', but serial in terms of consistently doing the same thing.

You know, to be quite frank, we're not intentionally saving lives, we're not at the cutting edge of some sort of medical science, we're actually opening our homes to people, we are welcoming people and creating experiences around the world. So, with that as our core, you have to approach business with a certain levity and an open heart and mind. I think that's hopefully what you experienced this morning.

Mok: *I did, it was lovely.*

What are you personally most proud of about Airbnb?

NR: I guess on a personal level I'm really proud of the fact that I can walk through the door every single day and be myself. I can be the authentic Nic. I don't have a game face, I don't have a strategy, I don't have any cards up my sleeve that I need to play. And I think that's because we have such an open culture at Airbnb. We are recognised for who we are, what we say and how we act, and I think that, being part of a global community, and a strong, strong internal culture, means that anybody that walks through the door can be themselves. And we all know that when you operate at your best, you are always being your authentic self. So yes, that's the one thing that I'm really proud of, that we've actually kind of built that culture that allows that to be the real thing.

Mok: *You said there was another thing, so one you're personally proud of, is there another?*

NR: I think second, in terms of the business, is the mission. I think if I have to take a real big step back and me personally, I think this mission... that mission allowed me to become part of this company as well, from being a host to stepping into the offices, to actually using those life skills for the betterment of other people within the office.

I'm proud of that because that mission is growing and evolving day in, day out and touching the lives of more and more people. So, yeah, it's difficult for a Brit to be so proud about things. It's something that I've learnt as well.

Mok: *And the final question: You've got a really exciting and engaging and playful culture at Airbnb. Any words of wisdom or advice you'd give to our listeners or readers around how they can create a culture as engaging as yours?*

NR: I think you've got to really, really attune to the staff and you've got to know your audience. So, as Ground Control, we are enablers of culture. We did have a saying way back when, which I think is really good. If you are sort of nurturing anyone in any field, 'Push for the sprint' and 'Support the marathon'. It's kind of like the Wright Brothers trying to get that aeroplane off the ground. Push, push, push, get them up in the air, and then you're there constantly underneath, ready to catch them when they fall. And I think for me, that's the best analogy when it comes to actually launching people into their own world.

CHAPTER FOUR
The Engine

Now you have a clear sense of Direction and your leadership is creating an Environment that can release the innovative potential of your workforce, you need to ensure that the right structures and processes are in place to support innovation and protect it from business-as-usual. Short-term results and business-as-usual activity will always seem more urgent and therefore demand more immediate attention. In order to ensure that innovation has the right focus, it is important to protect it and create a space for it among the pressure of the day-to-day running of a business – at The Innovation Beehive we call this the Engine.

Metrics

There is an elephant in the room when it comes to innovation: so many organisations do such a good job of avoiding measurement. In an age where there are so many metrics available – from balanced scorecard to NPS (net promoter score) – it is surprising that putting metrics around innovation still remains a challenge for many businesses.

Certainly, within the lack of hard numbers around innovation, there may be an element of 'metrics overload'; but if innovation is to have credibility and reach its full potential, it is vital that it is measured. I have seen a number of different ways to measure innovation efforts. Each business must choose a methodology that is right for it, but broadly speaking there are two overarching approaches: input measures and output measures.

Input measures you may consider are:

1. The number of employees trained in innovation tools and techniques

2. The number of ideas submitted to internal ideas tournaments or suggestion schemes

3. The amount of a leader's time spent focused on innovation efforts, as opposed to day-to-day activity

Output metrics you may consider are:

1. Percentage of new innovations in the pipeline

2. Percentage of customers engaging with new innovation offerings

3. Number of innovations coming from open source innovation efforts

I suggest that you adopt a blend of both input and output measurements. This holistic approach ensures that you are keeping a close eye on the conditions that need to be in place to drive innovation and the impact of the innovation itself.

Return on investment

Innovation efforts are not helped if they are initially measured by the same metrics used to measure day-to-day activities. Clayton Christensen has called this 'the innovator's dilemma', and he identified this as a major contributor to market disruption.[30]

Christensen argues that large incumbent market leaders tend to speak primarily to their current customers to ask for feedback and improvement suggestions. Current customers tend to be satisfied with the offering from the incumbent company and aren't able to predict the future or articulate what might be an unmet or future need. Alongside this, a small competitor can enter the marketplace and create an offering which may be at a lower price or spec but still meet an unmet customer need. We have seen this play out in the rise of the start-up community over the last few years. These small competitors are very adept at spotting an unmet need and working agilely to satisfy it.

The challenge for the large incumbent company is that the innovation created by the challenger or start-up does not, initially, offer a large enough market share or give the return on investment that may be required by the incumbent's shareholders, so it often rejects or ignores the potential of the new innovation. A start-up is often small enough to adapt and move at pace in response to customer feedback, which in turn means it is able to quickly create an offering which satisfies those needs – it does this by continually iterating and learning. This creates a perfect storm of the large incumbent ignoring the new innovation, and what it does for the customer, and the start-up obsessively responding to the customer and creating an offering that is more and more targeted to meeting the customer's needs.

It is in this climate that disruption occurs. The start-up's agility and responsiveness creates the disruption. Due to its size and legacy structures, the large incumbent struggles to catch up or adapt, and it often declines. Never has this been more apparent than with Kodak, who actually had the technology for digital photography but didn't exploit it sufficiently or understand that digital was not just a 'cute' edition to the market (as one senior manager described it) – it *was* the market.[31]

When I was leading an innovation team a few years ago in NYC, we worked with a large internet company that had initially established itself as the market leader, and the majority of customers held one of its domain email accounts. The client made money from the email account and was unwilling to see the market shift to free email. Its profits from its current offering were such a big part of its business that the client presumed user apathy would ensure its continued success, but the situation didn't play out like that. The business was eclipsed by other search engines that responded to and delivered what the customer wanted – alongside taking the incumbent's cash cow, free emails.

Christensen has recently argued that it is the traditional methods of measuring business success and opportunity that are stifling innovation. He claims that an over-reliance on traditional financial metrics has resulted in low experimentation rates and a focus on innovation around efficiency savings, resulting in a lack of innovation in many of the major US companies. He also argues that this 'capitalist's dilemma' is the result of a superabundance of capital, saying,

'We have entered a new environment of "capital superabundance".'[32]

As capital is cheap and traditional investment vehicles are failing to deliver significant growth, large investment institutions are looking for new vehicles in which to invest their capital. These institutions are increasingly investing directly into companies, seeing the potential for high ROI because of their innovation and growth record. However, whilst the investment institutions invest to capitalise on these innovations, their behaviour once they have invested can actually have a detrimental effect upon them.

Investors often measure success using metrics such as ROIC or RONA. This can lead them to continually put pressure on their portfolio, to deliver consistent short-term results. These short-term results are often created by efficiency innovations rather than new market or growth innovations. As a result, there is less focus on experimentation and risk. If innovation does manage to survive, it manifests itself in incremental tweaks.

The start-up revolution and Validated Learning

In the world of innovation, you cannot move without hearing about start-ups. One professional services client we worked with told us, 'Mention a start-up and it gets our clients very excited.'

Eric Ries codified what the start-up community does so well in his book *The Lean Startup*.[33] He identified that the start-up community is continuously iterating its product or service, often alongside its customers. This rapid testing and prototyping he called 'Validated Learning'.

Ries showed that successful start-ups identify a problem that needs to be solved and then create a rough prototype – a minimal viable product (MVP).[34] This MVP is then launched into the marketplace, with the full knowledge that it will change. He described this virtuous cycle as 'Build, Measure, Learn'.

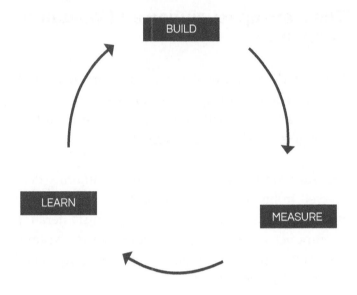

A significant contributing factor to the success of this approach is what Ries called 'Learn'. By continually going through this cycle, the start-up is able to gather 'validated learning' as its staff members keep experimenting with new iterations of their offering and learn more and more about how they can improve it to resolve the end user's need, pain or desire.

Each cycle of Build, Test, Learn may require a 'pivot' or slight change in execution, but the end goal and Direction remain the same. This virtual circle of continual improvement results in an offering that satisfies the end user's requirements better than anything else currently available in the market.

A few years ago, I was attending a dinner with one of the senior team at Tesla. He shared that the Tesla car is the only vehicle that actually gets better the longer you own it. He explained that once you buy a traditional car you are stuck with the technology in the vehicle, and this can become outdated quickly, whereas because Tesla's are run with software that is constantly updated, just like your phone, in eighteen months' time your car will be better than it was on the day you bought it. It updates based on the latest technology and customer data. It struck me that this is the very definition of validated learning.

A space for Validated Learning

Large-scale organisations must learn to prototype and gather feedback quickly to create the next iteration of their product or service. They need to build a process to gather validated learnings on their MVP.

Some organisations have created separate incubators within the business to focus on new market innovations. Coke has set up an entirely new business unit called Venturing and Emerging Brands to 'identify and nurture brands with billion-dollar potential'.[35] Its focus is on thinking five to ten years out on how the beverage market will evolve, and the unit has identified four stages in an innovation's life cycle:

1. Experimentation
2. Proof of concept
3. Pain of growth
4. Scale to win

Successes have included Zico coconut water and Honest Teas.

By laying out the four stages in the brand's life, Coke is building validated learning into its innovation process, thereby giving its people permission to experiment, fail and learn.

Incubators and Accelerators

The last few years have seen a tremendous rise in the number of Accelerators and Incubators. In 2017, global innovation foundation Nesta reported there were 205 Incubators and 163 Accelerators in the UK, representing £33 million of annual investment and supporting more than 3,500 new businesses a year.[36] What was particularly interesting was that more than half were corporate-funded.

Incubators

Incubators are typically housed in a physical space where start-up businesses or entrepreneurs are given offices on favourable rental terms. Their business ideas are supported with services such as training and access to a network. Incubators are often linked to universities or research facilities. Admission to an Incubator is on an individual basis, and typically there is no equity taken in the business. Business ideas are usually at a very early stage of development, with little proof of concept – hence they need to be protected or incubated.

Hasbro has supported online incubation programmes via its Hasbro Gaming Labs and Indiegogo collaboration; they allow Hasbro to share ideas and raise finance for new games through crowd funding. This structure allows the games that receive the most funding to receive $10,000 in prize money, as well as being invited to meet the Game Development Team at Hasbro. An early success with this approach was the funding and launch of the card game Irresponsibility featuring the character Mr Toast.

Accelerators

An Accelerator is very different from an Incubator. Admission to the former is generally via a highly selective application process. Accelerators are often sponsored by corporates and are cohort based; the services they provide include business planning, mentoring, idea pitching, prototyping and market testing. Unlike Incubators, no rent or membership fees are charged, and instead the Accelerator often takes a share of equity in the business.

Famous Accelerators include Y Combinator, which accepts approximately 2% of applications.[37] Notable alumni include Reddit, which was developed over sixteen months and bought by publishing group Condé Nast.

Seedcamp is a European Accelerator which exists to 'invest early in world-class founders attacking large, global markets and solving real problems using technology' (one notable alumnus is TransferWise).[38] It runs an entrepreneur boot camp with a week-long training programme in London. Seedcamp's point of differentiation is that it provides a cash injection from an investment fund of £20 million.

Barclays Bank is supporting Rise, which allows the bank to get in on the ground floor with innovators in the fintech community.[39] It provides an inspiring working environment and connection to global physical hubs in Europe, the US, Africa and Asia. It also houses the Barclays Accelerator – a thirteen-week programme for fintech start-ups, run in partnership with Techstars.

Rise is attempting to redefine financial services and shape the future of the industry by partnering with innovators. By giving them the resources and support they need, Rise plans to accelerate the development of new products and services which will keep Barclays at the forefront of the industry.

External partnering is proving particularly popular within the financial services industry. This may be, in part, because this industry operates in a highly regulated market, with significant media and public scrutiny. This environment can result in process-driven cultures, with an aversion to risk. This aversion to risk then manifests itself in a lack of experimentation and, at best, incremental innovation.

NatWest has partnered with an external agency to create Entrepreneurial Spark and established nine entrepreneur hubs across the UK. Alison Rose, CEO of commercial and private banking at NatWest, says:

> [We] want our staff to develop entrepreneurial
> mindsets to help them think differently and
> to problem solve in the same way business
> owners have to do on a daily basis. We have

set ambitious targets for the bank's unique Institute of Enterprise and Entrepreneurs-accredited Entrepreneurial Development Academy. To date, more than 6,000 people have volunteered and by the end of the year we anticipate over 8,500 employees will have joined the course, with a quarter of them achieving external accreditations.[40]

NatWest is using its Accelerator to deliver three parts of its Engine. Firstly, NatWest is supporting early-stage innovation; secondly, it's getting in on the ground floor of these early-stage innovations to stay aware of and keep close to potential market-disrupting innovations; and thirdly, NatWest is building the internal innovation capability of its people to think like a start-up by encouraging them to work alongside external entrepreneurs.

There are some potential risks of setting up an innovation centre. One organisation set up an entirely separate division and took twelve people with varying skills sets, backgrounds and tenures and challenged them to come up with the next big thing in their industry. They were taught a number of innovation skills and creative problem-solving techniques; however, the problem came when these individuals returned to their day jobs. They became disillusioned and felt that they were not able to use the new skills they had learnt, and many of them chose to leave.

We have also seen a business that set up a new division to come up with 'disruptive products and services for customers'. The staff in this division created some great ideas, but they failed to implement them. This was not because the ideas lacked insight or failed to respond to a genuine customer need; rather, the innovation team members had failed to work alongside the rest of the organisation as they developed their innovations. As a result, when they asked the markets around the world to test and prototype their ideas there was no incentive for them to do so. Their opinions had not been sought at either the Insight or the Ideation phase, and the ideas that were produced had no relation to the market's operational plan. There was also no funding available to test the ideas.

The result of this lack of integration between the innovation team and the markets led to some great ideas being abandoned. Worse still, a competitor had also identified the need for one of the ideas that the innovation team had produced. The competitor launched the idea in the marketplace first, which forced the bank that initially had the idea to make a defensive product launch and appear as a 'me too' in the marketplace.

Fidelity Labs – Scan, Try and Scale

One organisation that has a long-established separate innovation centre is Fidelity Investments. Over twenty years ago it founded Fidelity Labs in Boston, and now it has outposts all over the world.[41] Fidelity has a relentless focus on innovation, which is a major part of its $7 trillion success story. The lab grew out of the Fidelity Centre for Applied Technology, which was created in the 1990s to respond to the opportunities and threats from the new entity called 'the world wide web'.

The Innovation Lab has a mission to 'help Fidelity's businesses and clients to imagine the possibilities and benefits of new ideas and emerging technologies'. It does so in three ways – Scan, Try and Scale.

With 'Scan', Fidelity conducts research into emerging technology, invites thought leaders into the lab to share their points of view on what the future will hold, works with academic partners such as the D School and Harvard, and, increasingly, spends time with venture capital (VC) funds to identify emerging technology and opportunities in the start-up community. When I visited the lab in Boston, I was shown the work the staff there are currently undertaking to realise the potential of AR.

Part of the challenge of engaging investors in their portfolios is that it is not very exciting to look at bar charts or pie charts. Fidelity is aware of this, and has showcased a prototype for StockCity. This AR tool creates a virtual city from an investor stock portfolio.

The investments in different organisations are represented by the size and colour of the buildings. The investor is able to move around the city, comparing how their stocks are performing against each other. StockCity is intended to bring a portfolio to life and enable the investor to view the landscape of their investments in a physical form, therefore giving them a greater understanding of their investment's performance.

'Try' is Fidelity's experimental phase. Here Fidelity sets up new business incubators, develops technological proofs of concepts and runs hackathons, focused on completing a customer 'job to be done'. All this happens in a rapid, time-bound environment. Fidelity also operates Design Thinking Boot Camps, where a number of different stakeholders, including customers, come together over a week to solve an identified problem and build prototypes.

'Scale' is the final part of Fidelity Labs' innovation process. This is where Fidelity tests prototype MVPs with operational business units and develops patents. Again, this phase is run with real customers. Financial services are an incredibly regulated environment, and we often hear that it is difficult to innovate or test new innovations in such an environment. Fidelity Labs is set up as a separate entity from the main business and therefore avoids some of the more draconian regulation, which can slow down rapid iteration. Another approach, which works well for regulated organisations, is to engage a third-party supplier to carry out the testing phase. Subject to local legislation, they often have more flexibility than the regulated organisation and therefore avoid the limitations that regulation can impose.

Fidelity Labs says that a key factor in its success is the way it partners closely with the business units. This ensures that the areas in which the lab seeks to innovate are not the same as those of the business unit, and it therefore avoids some of the territorial behaviour we have seen in other organisations. Fidelity Labs is not in competition with the core business, which should be focused on delivering the current financial plan and thinking (at most) twelve to eighteen months ahead. The Innovation Lab is focused on three to five years ahead, and its innovations provide the business units with products and services to ensure their continued long-term growth and profitability. They may work on very different timescales, but they are very firmly innovation partners.

There are a number of reasons why an organisation may wish to set up or invest in an Accelerator. Nesta highlights four major ones:[42]

1. Rejuvenate corporate culture to create an entrepreneurial mindset among employees

2. Create an innovative brand to attract customers, business partners and future employees

3. Solve business problems quicker and at lower risk

4. Expand into future markets by assessing new capabilities/channels

Partnering with an external entity can be a great way to bring new ideas and fresh perspectives into your business organisation.

Making a separate innovation centre work

At the beginning of this book, I wrote that creating a process of innovation should not be your primary focus – instead, you should have a relentless focus on the outcome of your innovation efforts. Whether you set up a separate innovation Incubator or Accelerator will be dependent on a number of factors, such as funding and your organisation's approach to partnerships.

The most important thing to consider when deciding whether or not you partner externally is ensuring that any work done there is:

1. Aligned broadly with your Innovation Direction

2. Communicated at speed to the rest of the organisation, so they feel involved and do not reject the output

3. Does not compete against everyday business operations or improvements

We may find ourselves here with what I call 'the Incubator's dilemma' – keeping just enough distance to ensure that day-to-day business requirements do not limit your innovation efforts and ensuring that the organisation feels invested enough in your new innovations to allow MVPs to be tested.

The 'Jobs to be Done' and Design Thinking methodologies

At The Innovation Beehive, we sometimes meet clients who have been working for a long time to solve a problem. They tell us how they have come up with lots of ideas but that nothing has really landed or gained traction.

When we investigate a little further, we usually find that they do not have a clearly defined innovation methodology. At The Innovation Beehive, underpinning all of our work, are two approaches – the 'Jobs to be Done' theory and Design Thinking.

Jobs to be Done

Clayton Christensen developed the Jobs to be Done theory, and it is a very useful framework to adopt as you create your Innovation Engine.[43] Christensen says that innovation success can be predictable if you understand the job the customer really wants to be done. He argues:

> When we buy a product, we essentially 'hire' it to help us do a job. If it does the job well, the next time we're confronted with the same job, we tend to hire that product again. And if it does a bad job, we 'fire' it and look for an alternative.[44]

Your customer has a number of options for what product or service they can use or 'hire'. The key thing an innovator needs to understand is what job is the customer hiring your product or service to do – and it may not be what you think it is. This approach can free the innovator from the shackles of the product or technology that the business currently offers to the market. It allows them to truly step into the shoes of the end user and create an innovation that will do the job that needs to be done.

Let me give a real-life example to show the unexpected power and opportunity that can be uncovered by adopting a Jobs to be Done approach. Christensen worked with McDonald's to improve the sales of their milkshakes. In the past, they had created ideal customer personas and invited customers who bought milkshakes into focus groups to ask them what could be done with the product to encourage them to buy more. Taking this feedback, McDonald's invented new milkshake variations, but these innovations did not lead to a significant uplift in sales.

Christensen went back to the data and noticed that a significant per cent of milkshake sales were made before 8 am, and that the customer only bought this one item – crucially, to take away. He interviewed these customers and found that they had a long journey to work. This journey was dull, and the customer wanted to distract themselves from the monotony of the journey. The McDonald's milkshake was doing the job of 'entertaining' them on their commute to work.

There were a number of other products that could be 'hired' to do this task, but only the milkshake was able to entertain the customer for any significant length of time. A donut was nice, but it was eaten in minutes. A banana was a good option, but then, once you had eaten it, you had to work out what to do with the skin. The McDonald's milkshake took about twenty-three minutes to drink and therefore entertained them longer than any of the other alternatives the customer could have 'hired'.[45] The milkshake also filled them up so that they would not be hungry later on in the morning.

The McDonald's milkshake did the job better than any of the potential competitors that the customer could have hired to do the job. This realisation opened up a new competitor landscape for McDonald's; the company realised that it was competing not only with other milkshake providers such as Wendy's but also against bagels, bananas and Snickers bars. The actual market size was not the size of potential milkshake consumption; factoring in all the other competitors that could be hired to do the job, the market was seven times the size that McDonald's had originally imagined.

Christensen argues that understanding the job that the customer actually wants done, which may not be the job they are telling you about, is key to successful innovations. He says that the success of Ikea is not totally down to affordability but rather the fact that Ikea enables the customer to do the job of 'Getting me that piece of furniture today'[46]. Airbnb is not competing against hotels but rather doing the job of helping people live like locals and stay with friends. Customers don't want a hammer – they want a nail in the wall. The godfather of management, Peter Drucker, summed this up perfectly when he said, 'The customer rarely buys what the company thinks it is selling them.'[47]

Design Thinking

Creating a structure for innovation, such as Design Thinking, will enable you to better understand how your product or service is being experienced and used in your customer's life, and your innovation can then respond to that need. It will ensure you 'out-hire' the competition, every time.

Design Thinking is a 'human-centred approach' to innovation as it puts the end user at the heart of the process. Rather than thinking, 'What technology or product do I have that I can sell them?' Design Thinking enables you see the world through your customers' eyes and enables you to design products, services and experiences that can be easily hired to complete the job to be done.

Insight, Define, Ideate, Prototype, Test

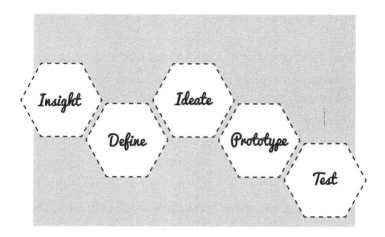

Insight

Insight is a first, and most crucial, stage in innovation. It requires you to step into the world of your end user and see it through their eyes. Observation and active listening are essential skills used to gather Insight. By seeing the world through your end user's eyes, you gain empathy into their lives and are able to identify their pain, need and desires. And this pain, need and desire is your opportunity for innovation.

To demonstrate true empathy with your end user, you must abandon all your preconceptions about them. Any assumptions you have about potential solutions must also be parked at this stage. This is a truly expansive way of operating. You are observing and listening. You want to understand the world from a different point of view.

Once you have seen the world this way, you are ready to move to the next stage, Define. This is where you will review your observations, look for patterns and turn these insights into value-creating opportunities.

Define

Once you have spent time with your end user, the second stage of Design Thinking invites you to look for emergent patterns in all you have observed and heard. We call these patterns Insights. The process calls for you to record and share what you have seen, looking for common patterns, emerging themes or 'truths'. At The Innovation Beehive, we call this 'Storytelling'.

It is tempting to assume that you know the problem your end user is experiencing. However, taking time to gather Insights enables you to identify the root causes of the problem. And the root cause may result in you solving a problem for the end user that you never knew existed.

Identifying the right problem to solve means that the solution you create will have a much better chance of being adopted. Many of the most disruptive innovations in the marketplace have emerged from taking time to Define the real problem to be solved – exactly what job needs to be done.

Netflix is a great example of an organisation that has innovated its way to world domination by understanding what job the customer needed to be done. Originally, Netflix posted CDs to your home, believing that the job the customer wanted done was 'I want to watch a movie'.

Netflix kept close to emerging tech (internet streaming) and user trends (YouTube), and it identified that the job the customer wanted done was to 'entertain me exactly when I want to be entertained'. Netflix began to do this by streaming movies and then moved into content creation and totally disrupted the entertainment industry. Blockbuster Video was the world leader in movie rental, but Blockbuster did not see that the job the customer wanted to be done was changing and that new technology offered a highly cost-effective way of delivering on the customer need.

Blockbuster Video went into administration in January 2013, and at that time Netflix's share price was US$165. In April 2018 it averaged US$320. Netflix was not some new start-up at that point – it was founded in 1997. What led to its success, and Blockbuster's demise, was understanding what job the customer wanted to be done.

Once you have clustered your Insights together and looked for repeating patterns, what will emerge will be the definition of the job to be done. Once you know the job to be done, you can Ideate your solution.

Ideate

The third stage of Design Thinking is where many organisations start their innovation efforts. They Ideate on what they think is the problem, without Insight or having Defined the job the end user wants done.

Ideation can take many forms but most often happens when a group of people come together with energy and commitment to explore potential solutions. At The Innovation Beehive, we teach a variety of tools and techniques to help our clients have great ideas. For more information on tools and techniques to help you have differentiated ideas, visit our website at www.innovationbeehive.com

It can often be extremely insightful to Ideate with your customers. However, whilst they might understand their needs better than anyone else, you should not only rely on your customers to help you come up with the truly ground-breaking ideas. This is because customers usually only focus on their current needs or what technology currently offers them.

This was best demonstrated to me when I was working with a mobile phone company in the US in the early 2000s. In focus groups, the company heard time and time again the customer stating that the most important things to them were signal clarity, not dropping calls and a small handset. This became the focus for the company's innovation efforts. And in the short term they had some significant success. But the business lived too much in the current world and did not have future sight.

The company failed to spot the smartphone opportunity or see that the mobile phone would become so much more than an oral communication device. By the time the company realised this, it was not able to recover quickly enough from the wounds inflicted by Apple's iPhone. The customer did not yet know that one day they would want their phone to be an entertainment suite, a taxi hailer or the myriad of other things that can now be done with a mobile phone.

Prototype

Once you have generated your potential solutions, Prototyping is where you create early concepts and visual representations. Prototyping brings an idea to life and allows you to gather feedback from your end user.

Prototyping is best done at speed – it is about creating a rough beta version of your solution. Don't be tempted to keep polishing the Prototype. Get it into the hands of your end user. We have seen examples where a Prototype is too polished, and this can have an impact on the genuineness of the feedback you will receive at the Test phase. Draw a picture, make a film on your phone or create a hand crafted Customer Journey. Don't overthink it – just do it.

Test

Once you have your rough Prototype, you need to share it with your end user to gather learning and feedback (your Validated Learning).

People are naturally polite. If they think you have spent a long time on something, they don't want to appear rude and tell you that they don't like it or that they wouldn't use it. By building your prototype at speed and making it slightly scrappy, you are inviting them to touch and feel it and imagine what it would be like to experience it. More importantly, you are signalling that what you are sharing is at an early stage and that you actively invite them to give negative comments, break it apart or reject it altogether.

Once you have tested your Prototype, you can iterate and make it better and more useful to your end user. This is the true meaning of 'Fail fast and learn':

Taking your Prototype, learning what doesn't work and changing it. At speed.

Where to place your focus

Design Thinking is a great way to focus your innovation efforts; however, I cannot over-emphasise the importance of the Insight and Define phases. It is tempting to rush in and go straight to idea generation; however, you will have lower-quality ideas and may not even solve the real problem.

This was brought home to me by one of The Innovation Beehive's clients. She told me about a chocolate manufacturer who identified a market potential in a developing country. A rising middle class, with more disposable income, had more money to spend on luxuries like chocolate. This company also had the technology to create chocolate bars that were significantly bigger than the local brand, using air.

When their products launched in market, they did not sell. The company re-examined their marketing and adjusted their packaging, but it still did not significantly impact on sales. Finally, as this project was of particular interest to the CEO, the leadership team went out to the market and spent time in consumers' homes, eating and talking about chocolate.

My client told me about one such interaction. As they sat on the sofa, the consumer handed her child a piece of chocolate and said, humorously (under her breath), 'Here, have some air'. My client's ears immediately pricked up, and she asked the consumer to repeat what she had said. Her host was mortified, but the client put her at ease and eventually the consumer replied: 'Well, you are Western. You can afford to pay for air. I want chocolate and not to have to pay for something that is free anyway.'

The chocolate company had failed to carry out the Insight phase successfully and had therefore made assumptions about the consumer which were wrong. The company had defined the problem to be solved as the size of the chocolate bar, which led them to produce a product that did not appeal to its target market. In fact, it felt like the consumers were being ripped off.

Focus on the Insight and Define stage and you will identify where the real value-creating opportunity lies. Go straight to Ideate and you will only be working with your personal assumptions and could, like the chocolate manufacturer, come up with a new product that fails to provide what your end user really wants.

The Engine summary

It is not enough to simply talk innovation. You must be able to measure it and have the structures in place to enable it to happen. Day-to-day, operating financial metrics can often discourage innovation, and by applying a short-term lens to new opportunities businesses run the risk of killing a project before it has time to prove its worth. Different measurement criteria should be applied to innovation to encourage experimentation and risk taking.

Looking outside the organisation for inspiration can provide a fresh perspective and re-invigorate corporate cultures or individuals who have become used to business-as-usual and are unable to see a challenge from a fresh and alternative perspective. Formal partnerships, supporting new talent or ideas with structures such as Incubators or Accelerators and developing open source platforms, can all result in the injection of fresh thinking into the organisation.

Having a systematic approach to innovation, such as Design Thinking, ensures that you do not rush too quickly to generate ideas. Google says that 'Creativity loves constraint',[48] and by ensuring you have a framework for your innovation efforts you are able to drill down into the job to be done for your end user.

Whilst it is vital to bring in fresh thinking from outside and to fully immerse yourself into the life of your end user, your greatest ideas may already be within your business, and you should also look to the creative potential of your people to solve your innovation dilemmas. In the next chapter, I will reveal how you can Enable your people to share and generate ideas and realise the potential that already exists within your organisation.

ACTIVITY: REFLECTING UPON YOUR ORGANISATION

Consider the following questions:

1. How do you currently measure innovation success?

2. What metrics could you use to measure both input and output?

3. How do you iterate your innovations and ensure that learnings from users are incorporated rapidly into your prototype?

4. How do you ensure that your innovation teams keep close to the broader business, so that their innovation outputs are understood and trialled?

5. Who could you partner with to ensure fresh perspectives and ideas are brought inside your organisation?

6. What is your framework for innovation?

7. What job do you think your product or service fulfils in your end user's life?

Interview with Magdalena Krön, Director of Barclays Bank-supported Rise Accelerator, the Rise Group

Mok: *How did you go from your own experience as a start-up, to then helping start-ups, to then the Rise Accelerator?*

MK: So, that was a quite natural transition, so I went to a lot of events during this role and kind of saw also what else is missing for start-ups. So, if you tick the seed funding or you tick the funding box, the start-up needs talent but also customers, and customers like a big corporate is often a very good thing for a company because they get the traction, they get the proof of concept, they get the feedback they need to be able to scale their product.

Well, I started looking for new opportunities, and I met the head of design and digital office at Barclays, and he pitched this brilliant project to me about building out a platform for entrepreneurs where you would have physical locations in many different parts of the world that could then kind of establish and create an ecosystem and a community that would help the bank to innovate better. It would help the start-ups to grow and scale their business, and it would also help the bank kind of take their business forward and connect our clients and connect our banking services with this network.

Mok: *Tell me a little bit about the work you do, particularly with the start-ups here. So, what support does Rise and Barclays give to start-ups?*

MK: I head up Rise London, which is our largest site. We currently have five sites globally. In the space here at Rise we have forty-eight fintech companies, so we're really focusing on fintech innovation and what will transform the future of financial services. Bringing the best and the brightest entrepreneurs into one space, we hope to create a cluster of the most interesting innovations and products and services that are being built today in the different areas of financial services.

Our entrepreneurs and founders get a network that they can operate in and can help each other grow. But we also create… We also link in a lot of the bank's resources, and our core capabilities and intelligence which can be anything from industry expertise, understanding of how to work with regulators, we have a VC network that we can connect them into. We have a client network that we can connect them into.

But essentially why a lot of the companies come here is because they're all interested to work with Barclays as a bank.

Mok: *What's in it for Barclays? Why does Barclays choose to support this, what does it get out of it by creating this partnership?*

MK: Innovation is the big thing. We, as a bank, can see that technology is going to play a much bigger role in the way we interact with our customers, and even though we're quite on the forefront as a bank, of how we think of our digital propositions, we still have a long way to go. We see that there are incumbents coming in and changing our business models and making some of our business models obsolete. And now, with all the new companies coming in, the consumer has a wider range of options.

And also these new incumbents have a different interaction with their customers – they make it really simple, which is what we can learn from these companies and collaborate with them and create with these companies. That's essentially what we want to do. We're not in this space to steal ideas, we're here to actually see how can we identify these transformative technologies that really resonate well with customers and consumers, and how can we look at bringing that thinking into our product development?

Mok: *One of the key elements of The Innovation Ecosystem is the Engine, and we strongly recommend that organisations partner with external businesses, particularly the start-up community. If someone is sitting in a large corporate now and they are thinking about* *partnering with externals, what advice would you give them as they start to create their partnership strategy?*

MK: So, I think there are two pieces of advice. The first one is just to simply start and try to test and learn as much as possible in that process, and that could be taking different strategies around acquiring, co-creating, simple partnerships or just making sure that you get as much experience as possible.

The second piece in this process is to make sure that you get the business to follow along. Open up a lot of conversation, communicate what you're doing, tell the stories about what you're doing and how you're doing it. Because it's a long-term game, it's not just for the next six or twelve months, this is something that you have to establish over many, many years, and changing the culture of people inside the business will help you in the long term to actually make a difference and promote these external partnerships, which really adds more innovation into your business.

Mok: *Great. Well, it sounds like a really exciting place at Rise, I know it's a very exciting place, buzzing when I came in this morning. What do you love about your job?*

MK: I love that I get to work with really passionate people, both the entrepreneurs and the founders, who really have identified a problem that they strongly believe that they can solve, and they're building some awesome products and just going for it. So that kind of, being around the go-getter mentality is really exciting on a daily basis.

And then also to be able to connect these companies into opportunities with the bank and our clients and partners.

CHAPTER FIVE

The Enablers: Building The Innovation Capability Of Your People

Workplace contexts

When you walk into an office building, you can often sense the energy of the place. When I visit Google's London Campus, it buzzes with energy and creativity. You observe people interacting, giving eye contact, smiling at each other and genuinely looking like they are happy to show up for work.

Other offices I visit are not so much fun. You know what I am talking about – workplaces where there is silence, where notices from 'Management' tell you to do this or do that, and it feels like people are expected to leave their personality at the front door when they come in.

These two different working environments can have a profound effect on innovation. In all of my years of working in HR and innovation, I have never observed an organisation where people who are unengaged can come up with significant innovations.

Over recent years, employee satisfaction surveys and awards such as Great Place to Work have moved very clearly onto the management agenda. MBA programmes now all contain a module on People Management. This focus on people isn't about altruism; it is a business imperative. I remember my old Human Resources Director for a well-known retailer telling me: 'People stuff isn't about being nice – it's necessary.'

Put simply, an engaged workforce will be more likely to try and solve your customers' problems and go that extra mile to find a solution. An unengaged workforce will only complete the tasks that make up their job description, and they will be disinclined to use their own initiative or demonstrate an incremental effort. An unengaged workforce is an uninnovative workforce.

A few years ago, The Innovation Beehive was asked by a client to help them improve their customer-service experience. When we first started the conversation, the focus of the project was on delivering new customer-service training. However, when we conducted our Insight and looked at other organisations that delivered a consistent and delightful customer experience, we realised that they focused on the employee experience first. By focusing on the employee first, they created an engaged and motivated workforce, who in turn deliver great customer experiences.

We took this insight and, rather than create a service-training programme, we developed a culture change programme. This programme focused on taking care of the employees so that they could take care of the customer. The results have been wonderful. Employee engagement has increased,[49] customer compliments have increased and there have been promising sales increases.

The lesson is clear. Everyone knows you should smile at a customer, but it won't happen unless the organisation has given the employee a reason to smile. That sense of being taken care of and feeling appreciated by the organisation has a direct impact on the level of care and appreciation a customer receives.

Harvard Business School has summed up the link between employee engagement and business success in the Profit Chain Equation. This equation establishes relationships between profitability, customer loyalty, and employee satisfaction, loyalty, and productivity. The links in the chain (which should be regarded as propositions) are as follows: Profit and growth are stimulated primarily by customer loyalty. Loyalty is a direct result of customer satisfaction. Satisfaction is largely influenced by the value of services provided to customers. Value is created by satisfied, loyal, and productive employees. Employee satisfaction, in turn, results primarily from high-quality support services and policies that enable employees to deliver results to customers.[50]

Put simply, if you engage your workforce, they will deliver engaging end-user experiences, which will drive loyalty and repeat business. This will increase sales and deliver better profitability as existing customers are more profitable.

This link between your employee satisfaction and business results is a key factor in the fourth element of The Innovation Ecosystem. The world's most innovative organisations put such a high premium on employee engagement because they know that a satisfied workforce is one which is Enabled to innovate.

Motivating your people to release their potential

I believe that one of the best approaches to understanding how to engage your people can be found in the work of the behavioural scientist Daniel Pink. He argues that, 'There is a mismatch between what science knows and what business does.' [51]Pink references a 1960s behavioural science experiment called 'the Candle Problem', which presented the following dilemma:[52]

Two groups of participants were asked to attach a candle to a wall in such a way that the wax did not drip onto the table.

Each group was given:

• One candle

• One box of thumbtacks

• One book of matches

The two groups were incentivised in two different ways. The members of the first group were told that they would be timed, to establish norms around how long it took to complete the task. The second group was financially incentivised to complete the task in the fastest possible time. The group that was financially incentivised to complete the task took on average three and a half minutes longer than the other group.

You might be thinking, 'How could that be possible?' Taking the traditional management approach, the financial incentive should sharpen creativity and accelerate performance, yet 'it does just the opposite... the contingent motivators, if you do this you will get that, for a lot of tasks, they don't work or often they do harm'.[53]

This has profound implications for business, when viewed through the lens of the types of work and thinking that will be required to succeed in the twenty-first century. Pink argues that many businesses are still operating its incentives and engagement programmes with an industrial mindset when repetitive tasks or highly codified and repetitive working patterns make up the majority of jobs. This segmented type of work responded well to small, incremental and often monetary reward.

In the twenty-first century, we live in VUCA times – volatile, uncertain, complex and ambiguous.[54] Traditional systematic Tayloristic thinking around cause and effect will not help us to innovate. Old ways of rewarding and old ways of working will not result in the innovations required where the pace of change is continually increasing.

In uncertain times there is no manual to refer to for the 'right answer'. It is increasingly difficult to even identify the root cause of a problem. If your employee reward systems are built on the belief that there is one right answer and one right way of working, you will be left behind.

New challenges will require increased collaboration and experimentation. Experts will no longer hold all the answers. VUCA times will require businesses to release the full potential of their people so that they can come together and bring their collective thinking to solve each new challenge.

Repetitive tasks can be outsourced or replaced entirely by AI and emerging tech platforms; many roles now require more creativity and personal decision making – right-side-brain activities as opposed to left-side-brain activities. Pink says that the mechanistic, reward-and-punishment approach often doesn't work and can actually do harm. He argues that an employee needs to be paid what they consider to be fair for the job you are asking them to do – pay enough 'to take the issue of money off the table'. After that, employers need to appeal to extrinsic motivators of:

1. Autonomy – Our desire to be self-directed; it increases engagement over compliance

2. Mastery – The urge to get better skills

3. Purpose – The desire to do something that has meaning and is important, in the service of something larger than ourselves

The importance of these three extrinsic motivators can be seen in the success of Wikipedia as opposed to Encarta. The contributors to Wikipedia receive no financial incentive for their work, in contrast to the salaried employees who worked on Encarta. Wikipedia is maintained by volunteers, whereas Encarta – now extinct – was a business product created by Microsoft. Wikipedia was built for fun, by volunteers, because they believed in the project.[55]

By the time of Encarta's closure announcement (April 2009), Encarta had about 62,000 articles, most behind a paywall, while the English Wikipedia had over 2.8 million articles in open access. By the time of Encarta's closure (December 2009), the English Wikipedia had over 3.1 million articles.[56]

You have already read in Chapter Two about the importance of Purpose – giving your employees the duvet-chuck moment. This is even more important in light of Pink's argument that the best way to Enable your people to perform is to give them the tools to complete the job and then let them thrive. He calls this Motivation 2.0, and it is best summed up by the author:

Carrots and sticks are so last century. Drive says for twenty-first century work, we need to upgrade to autonomy, mastery and purpose.[57]

Wikipedia's contributors have clear sense of purpose. Encarta's contributors just had a salary. To really turn your employees into innovators, you must consider how you can best engage them to deliver innovations and customer delight. Traditional management approaches won't enable you to compete in VUCA times, and those organisations that will win in the twenty-first century are the ones that understand what will best motivate their employees to succeed.

Structures as Enablers

The danger with implementing a new structure is that it can become a blocker to creativity. It can become another hurdle for your employees to overcome. However, structures can also act as Enablers for innovation.

Ed Catmull is the President of Pixar Animation and Disney Animation, and he has created a structure to support creativity and innovation. I had the privilege to hear him speak on how he implemented a simple structure to release the potential of his people in both organisations. He implemented a 'Braintrust'.[58] The Braintrust is a peer-to-peer group that meets to give honest notes on a project. It removes the power structures and egos that so often exist in an organisation and encourages real collaboration. Ed Catmull says that in the Braintrust, 'magic happens'.[59]

In these meetings, the director of a project presents their work and then their peer group members are free to comment with 'candour', whilst watching out carefully for personal dynamics. This structure enables people to see their project through the eyes of others, who all have a common goal to try and improve the project: 'Ego disappears from the room; all attention is on the problem… ideas come and go, and people are not attached to them. It's not about them – it's about the idea.'[60]

Catmull argues that the flow of information and ideas should not mirror a traditional organisational structure. So often in business we are concerned with getting people up to speed so they don't get surprised in a meeting with a new piece of information. At Pixar and Disney, Catmull has created a culture where it is OK to find out new information in a meeting because he believes that communicating according to the organisation structure will result in layers of management slowing ideas down and frustrating the creative process – what he calls 'sand in the gears'.[61]

You could argue that the Braintrust is just another mechanism for giving and receiving feedback. And you would be partially right. As Catmull explained to *Fast Company*:

> There are two key differences, as I see it. The first is that the Braintrust is made up of people

with a deep understanding of storytelling, who usually have been through the process themselves. While the directors welcome critiques from many sources, they particularly prize feedback from fellow storytellers. The second difference is that the Braintrust has no authority. The director does not have to follow any of the specific suggestions. After a Braintrust meeting, it is up to him or her to figure out how to address the feedback. Giving the Braintrust no power to mandate solutions affects the dynamics of the group in ways I believe are essential.[62]

This means that not only does the feedback come from a very credible and trusted source (your peer) but, because the Braintrust has no direct influence, all feedback is given from a place of positive intention.

Enabling start-ups in large organisations

Johnson and Johnson (J&J) have a long-established Incubator called JLABS which works with healthcare start-ups and enables them to have the best possible opportunity to deliver upon their early-stage promises. They have created JPALs to respond to a frequently occurring problem with large organisations and their incubators. JPALs 'act as mentors to our resident companies, providing knowledge, connections, and support in order to help them succeed'.[63]

I attended an event at the world-famous Accelerator MassChallenge in Boston and heard about the great work J&J are doing to integrate start-ups into the corporate body. They have created a 'JPAL' who is there to connect the dots in J&J for a start-up and to ensure that the work and its iterations are aligned to J&J's strategy. He believes that this is a significant Enabler to building sustained partnerships that create value for both sides.

Ideas can come from anywhere

If you are going to ask your people to generate ideas to solve your business challenge, you must give them the skills to do it. You would not ask someone to drive a car without giving them driving lessons, and most people have received at least a cursory training session on their job at an induction. Yet in business we often expect people to have good ideas without any training. Shouldn't we Enable them first?

Adobe has a structured innovation capability-building scheme called the Kickbox programme. This programme began life as an internal resource but is now open to anyone to complete online. It is 'designed to increase innovator effectiveness, accelerate innovation velocity, and measurably improve innovation outcomes'.[64] It has six stages, starting with Inception (Insight) and finishing with Iterate (Pitching the idea). Kickbox encourages individuals to work on ideas, without the approval hoops which so often characterise large corporates. Participants receive a 'red box' with all the tools and material they need to move through the six stages. They are empowered to rapidly prototype and test as each red box contains a pre-loaded Citi credit card with a $1,000 on it.[65]

Whilst Adobe has created a DIY training Enabler to encourage innovation, Fidelity Labs is much more interventional. The latter collaborated very early on with the D School at Stanford in some of the very first Design Thinking teaching programmes. The collaborators have taken this approach back to Fidelity Labs and have trained thousands of their associates in this methodology. They say:

> It gives teams a process and a vocabulary to use when addressing ambiguous problems. Its fundamental value lies not in the number of pipe cleaners used or stokes done in a workshop, but in its ability to change how people approach problems.

> Our team believes that the pursuit of new opportunities calls for the adoption of certain mindsets. Our team aims to cultivate a

human-centred approach and a culture of prototyping through Design Thinking so that everyone at Fidelity creates the best products and services based on customer need. Fidelity Labs has long held a customer-centered and experimental approach – and Design Thinking helps us to up our game that much more.[66]

Fidelity Labs also runs emerging-technology clubs, similar to a book club. Each 'club' hosts quarterly meet-ups, and they focus on areas such as Blockchain, AI or Big Data. Experts and innovators in each area are invited to Fidelity to share their knowledge and experience with anyone at Fidelity who wants to attend. This not only supports phase one of Fidelity's innovation process (Scan), but, since those associates who are interested in new things tend to gravitate towards the club, the meet-ups can also act as a recruiting ground for future talent to join the Lab.

Cisco enables internal innovation capability with its 'Adventure Kits'. These kits support Cisco's Innovate Everywhere Challenge.[67] This bi-annual challenge uses a clear Strategic Table of Elements to focus the organisation on key strategic opportunity areas.[68] The whole philosophy of the programme is to disrupt Cisco to ensure the start-up spirit is thriving.

The key objectives of the Innovate Everywhere Challenge are to:

1. Create game-changing value for customers, partners and employees

2. Develop entrepreneurship skills and an innovation culture at Cisco

3. Enhance employee experience, empowerment and collaboration across all functions

4. Reinforce Cisco's 'innovator' brand to attract, develop and retain talent

The results of a recent challenge were astounding, with 48% of employees engaged in the challenge in some way and more than 1,110 ideas submitted. Combining individual efforts to create 'innovation teams' was actively encouraged – to the extent that around 50% of the submissions were from teams. More than 45,000 votes were cast, and the winner announced during a ninety-minute, live broadcast finale, where three teams received what they needed to implement their ideas. This included three months to work on the idea, a personal financial reward, funding to develop the idea further, extensive technology support and mentoring.

What has worked so well at Cisco is that this innovation programme is supported by capability-building initiatives, including training and coaching.

It is focused on clearly articulated objectives (the Direction), encourages collaboration and cross-functional working (the Environment), and there are clear rewards in place to incentivise participation (the Engine).

With such high employee participation, the Innovate Everywhere Challenge creates a movement of engaged employees, all of whom feel empowered to make a difference and all of whom feel they have a voice. Cisco now showcases this programme as part of its Employee Value Proposition and its Great Place to Work submission.

Innovation Sprints

Whilst the Cisco programme is run over an extended period of time, innovation can also be enabled over much shorter timescales.

Atlassian is a software development company based in Australia that runs 'Shipit days'. It is also a winner of the Australian Best Place to Work Award. Atlassian's twenty-four-hour Shipit innovation tournament focuses the whole organisation on solving customers' problems, creating new products and solving business challenges.

Shipits are all about creating amazing ideas. They are an intense manifestation of Daniel Pink's belief in the impact of autonomy on performance. At Shipits, individuals are tasked with finding other people with whom to form teams. At the end of twenty-four hours, the teams give a three-minute presentation on their idea. The grand finale is broadcast into multiple rooms across the business.

The rules of Shipit are simple:

1. Work on whatever you want

2. Assemble your crew

3. You've got twenty-four hours. Go!

Shipit encourages everyone in the organisation to down tools for twenty-four hours in order to innovate. It is, in essence, developing innovation capability through action. The teams solve the challenges set by the Direction, with competitive fun.

Whilst Shipit days encourage mass collaboration and frantic activity, innovation can also be incorporated into already existing structures such as learning and development (L&D) programmes.

Learning frameworks to support innovation

NBC Universal (owned by Comcast Cable) uses its L&D framework – the Talent Lab – to create a culture of innovation, build capability and generate ideas for growth. An example of one of their development programmes is CASE, where cross-functional middle management work together to solve a live business issue.

Innovation capability is also developed in more senior leaders. NBC's DRIVE programme takes a group of twenty-five executives and focuses them on one business challenge that needs re-thinking. They visit Comcast's Silicon Valley Incubator and meet with external strategic partners to gain fresh thinking and new experiences. This can then be applied to the specific challenge they are faced with on the programme, as well as used in their day jobs long after the programme has finished. 'When you combine the aspirations of people to do better for themselves with the interest of the business, it is a wonderful thing,' says Bill Strahan, EVP of HR at Comcast Cable.

We can see from the work at NBC that, to be effective, innovation capability does not have to happen in one energetic burst. Lloyds Banking Group is also developing its workforce's innovation capability in a number of creative ways. These include Digital

Espressos, where external experts are invited to share their thinking. The Group's graduate population is trained on idea-generation techniques using remote technology and at an annual big brainstorming session. Meanwhile, solutions to specific challenges are captured from employees using an idea-management system. The latter encourages comment and participation and rewards employees for ongoing engagement.

The Enablers summary

The Enablers is the final – and often the most over-looked – part of The Innovation Ecosystem. Traditional reward methods, created for the industrial work-place, need to be re-thought in increasingly uncertain times in order to fully release the innovation potential of your people. Without the skills to innovate, you cannot expect your people to have great ideas. It is not simply enough to set the Direction, encourage the Environment and put structures in place to create the Engine.

There are a number of ways you can develop your internal innovation capability and Enable your employees to become innovators – from formal idea-generation programmes to blending innovation priorities into your L&D agenda. These Enablers create a sense of empowerment among your people, making them feel responsible and accountable for their own and the organisation's future success. This leads to greater employee engagement and the releasing of your workforce's creative potential to solve your business challenge.

Your employees become innovators.

ACTIVITY: REFLECTING UPON EMPLOYEE ENGAGEMENT

Reflect upon the following questions:

1. How might you explain to your leaders the link between employee engagement and user satisfaction?

2. Have you communicated the Purpose and impact of your team members' roles so that they feel they are making a difference and achieving more than the constituent parts of a job description?

3. Do your people understand how their jobs contribute to a Purpose that encompasses more than just making money?

4. What behaviours do your current reward mechanisms recognise? Do they encourage experimentation?

5. What structures could you put in place that encourage your people to put their ideas forward?

6. How could you train your people on creating ideas and your leaders on encouraging them?

Interview with Will Reddaway, Group Head of Innovation at J Murphy & Sons

Mok: *Tell me a little bit about your role; you're Group Head of Innovation at J Murphy & Sons.*

WR: The role initially was fairly broad. It was: stimulate an innovative culture. The second thing was to embed a culture of collaboration and empowering our staff to behave differently; train – either directly or indirectly – our staff to understand and appreciate different types of innovation and what innovation is and how it can be construed and what it entails, try to maximise funding opportunities to stimulate growth by stimulating knowledge and opportunities, tap into SMEs, small and medium enterprises, start-ups, try to give them a way into our business to actually create a bit of disruption, but also just to seek out new ways of working, new experience.

Then, penultimately, develop an academic network, so spread the tentacles out to as many universities as possible to come and work with us, for us to get there, to share their skills, their knowledge, new advances in concrete, steel, fabrication or whatever, to stimulate how we work and understand that actually this way of pouring concrete can be completely revolutionised if we add this compound to it, for example. But if we don't have that knowledge, we can't do that.

Lastly is to maximise our R&D tax claims, which is something that as an industry we're not very good at doing in the first place. That creates a self-fulfilling cycle of funding and a pot of money for proof of concepts. We're never going to spend millions of pounds on buying businesses with this money. It's there to either buy people's time, to de-risk a programme, to create a sandbox, to try something on a live project, to pay for a bit of IT or a bit of equipment to try something. Again, it's to understand our proof of concept, whether it's capable, whether it aligns with our ten-year plan, aligns with our values and our strategic drivers, and whether or not it actually does what it says on the tin before we deploy it.

Mok: *It's a broad role, lots of pieces there. If you had to choose one, what's the one piece that you enjoy the most?*

WR: I think the thing I enjoy most is seeing that realisation in people's eyes that what they're doing is actually contributing to our Innovation Ecosystem, to our innovation behaviours, and creating value for the business.

Because a lot of people do their job, they say, 'I come in, I'm an accountant, you crunch your numbers, you do your value bit by providing the data the company needs to make decisions, business intelligence,' but if you're doing something which adds more value it doesn't always get appreciated. But then I think what I offer is that sounding board and that bit of reflection, so people realise, 'Well actually I'm adding more value than I realised, I did something that actually is considered ahead of the game or transformational.'

Mok: *One of the things you talked about there is, 'We passionately believe about unlocking and releasing the potential of people at work, and the ideas are in people, and money is on the table in organisations, you just need to release people's creative potential, their innovative potential, and they can come up with the ideas to solve your problem.' What you're talking about there is enabling people to do that. Can you tell us a little bit about how J Murphy & Sons enable people to become involved in innovation and feel that their contribution is valued?*

WR: I wanted to create that stimulation for people to ask questions. The Innovation Foundation was based on an open systematic approach to delivering innovation – process procedures but ownership and accountability. So, the thing I made clear from the beginning when I started with the whole of the C Suites, the directors and the leadership team, is that I need your support, you need to bring it in on the agenda. It should no longer be a tick-box exercise. It needs to be brought in, believed in and actually can realise some value.

I then started from the ground roots-level up as well. Because in my opinion, in my experience, innovation cannot be tendered, it has to be nurtured, it's grown from the bottom and nurtured from the top.

What we've created is a very, very transparent open innovation platform where all levels would put their ideas in and you will get directors and even sometimes members replying to people saying, 'That's a fantastic idea.' Straight away that credibility goes up for the programme because people think I'm being taken seriously. But just to really put it into perspective, we've recently funded one of our first ideas which will be on our public website, Innovation Edge, but it's effectively an in-house eBay for Murphy because when we buy materials for a job we'll sometimes over-deliver or over-order or bring the wrong stuff.

Mok: *Tell me about your Champion network.*

WR: In a building like this, for example, you'll have first aiders, you'll have fire wardens and so on. It's a discretionary role. You don't have to do it, but you do it because you feel you want to add some value to or help out the business, for example. In our industry we have diversity champions, we've got STEM ambassadors and they're all really important.

And I kind of feel, people take on these voluntary roles all the time, so would people be up for being an innovation champion? We've got champions at all levels, from heads to operative level, and they've all been given the time to take some time out to go and work, do a workshop with me or whatever.

Mok: *What's their role? What do they do?*

WR: Their roles are pretty simple. They're an ambassador for innovation, they need to know what innovation is about, so they need to understand our Innovation Strategy. They need to know examples of innovation at Murphy so that they can relate to other people, helping people bring ideas onto our innovation portal, putting innovation as an agenda item in their meetings that they attend, making sure that toolbox – which are morning briefing meetings that you have out on site – that an innovation piece is put in.

But they are also a naïve resource; they invite themselves to meetings that might not be anything to do with their discipline but just to try to stimulate opportunities as well. And they disrupt, in the positive way, meetings and operations to actually add some value. So, we've got a slowly growing network of innovation challengers. We're up to about seventy now.

Mok: *What do you think the impact has been of enabling them to be innovation champions and making the resources available to the rest of the organisation?*

WR: Belief that actually it's taken seriously. They now feel, 'If I want to go to an innovation meeting or attend an innovation workshop or go to meet someone like you', for example, and they have to take half a day off that's not seen as a waste of time.

151

Mok: *If someone sitting here listening to this and they are trying to develop their Innovation Strategy, what three pieces of advice would you give them as they start to formulate their strategy?*

WR: Just three pieces? Firstly, you have to have a huge amount of strength and tenacity because there will be a lot of naysayers, there will be a lot of people who don't understand it, so being very, very, not bloody-minded – that's probably too far – but tenacious and strong and resolute in your beliefs is key.

Secondly, I think understanding the business, getting under the skin of the business, not trying to deliver an Innovation Strategy within two weeks, three weeks, get a feel for business, understand the senior leadership team, understand the junior members of the team, understand the whole business as a whole, try and vicariously absorb everything that's happening in the business so that when you create an Innovation Strategy or an innovation capability you can address key issues for everyone and there'll be something that people can relate to.

Lastly, I think you need to try if you can to bring in a cultural understanding of what innovation is, with maybe some training.

Conclusion

I have worked with organisations large and small, to help them create sustainable innovations which continue to delight their employees and customers. I have come to understand that a single intervention, such as an idea-generation scheme, can't deliver sustainable innovation. One activity may result in a small spike in ideas or engagement, but it will quickly disappear as day-to-day business activities take priority and the latest management intervention falls off the radar.

Successful organisations avoid this by creating an Innovation Ecosystem. This ecosystem turbocharges efforts and ensures they are sustained. The Innovation Ecosystem provides the framework for creating an entire innovation system within your organisation. It pulls on all the levers that drive change – strategy, leadership, engagement, structure, finance, operations and capability.

It is important that you create The Innovation Ecosystem that is right for you. Take inspiration from the great strategy articulation at Cisco, the culture at Airbnb, Rise's agile working style, and J Murphy & Sons, innovation roles; but, ultimately, you must create an ecosystem that will work with your own culture and customer requirements.

One of the best pieces of advice I heard whilst writing this book was from Magdalena Krön at Rise – 'Just start.' And that is my last piece of advice for you.

Start your journey here:
https://scorecard.innovationbeehive.co.uk

Notes

1   J. Clark, 'Google: At scale, everything breaks', ZDNet, (22 June 2011), www.zdnet.com/article/google-at-scale-everything-breaks (accessed 11 November 2018).

2   C. M. Christensen, *The Innovator's Dilemma: When New Technologies Cause Great Firms to Fail* (Boston, MA: Harvard Business Review Press, 1997).

3   J. Dyer, H. B. Gregersen, and C. M. Christensen, *The Innovator's DNA: Mastering the Five Skills of Disruptive Innovators* (Boston, MA: Harvard Business Review Press, 2011).

4   A. Brownsell, 'Apple retains crown as world's most valuable brand as Facebook value sinks', Campaign (4 Oct. 2018), www.campaignlive.co.uk/article/apple-retains-crown-worlds-valuable-brand-facebook-value-sinks/1494790 (accessed 13 November 2018).

5   T. J. Peters and R. H. Waterman Jr., *In Search of Excellence: Lessons from America's Best Run Companies* (London: HarperCollins, 1982).

6   L. Carroll, *Alice's Adventures in Wonderland and What Alice Found There* (London: Penguin Classics, 1998), p. 56.

7   'Facebook IPO: Letter from Mark Zuckerberg', *The Telegraph* (1 Feb. 2012), www.telegraph.co.uk/finance/newsbysector/mediatechnologyandtelecoms/9055830/Facebook-IPO-Letter-from-Mark-Zuckerberg.html (accessed 11 November 2018).

8   The formation of Alphabet Inc. was announced by Larry Page in this blog post 'G is for Google' (Official Google blog post, 10 Aug. 2015), https://googleblog.blogspot.co.uk/2015/08/google-alphabet.html (accessed 13 November 2018).

9   Page, 'G is for Google'.
10 L. Page and S. Brin, '2004 Founders' IPO Letter', Alphabet Investor Relations (2004), https://abc.xyz/investor/founders-letters/2004/ipo-letter.html (accessed 11 November 2018).
11 M. Ringel, A. Taylor, and H. Zablit, 'The Most Innovative Companies 2015: Four factors that differentiate leaders', The Boston Consulting Group Reports (December 2015).
12 M. Randall, 'Table of Strategic Elements', Disruptive Influence (25 Apr. 2012), www.markrandall.com/table-of-strategic-elements (accessed 11 November 2018).
13 T. Kneen, 'Watch it grow: Cisco's innovation ecosystem', Cisco UK & Ireland blog post (16 Oct. 2017), https://gblogs.cisco.com/uki/watch-it-grow-ciscos-innovation-ecosystem (accessed 13 November 2018).
14 H. Romanski, 'Cisco's 200th Acquisition – a Tradition of Advancement, Disruption and Growth', Cisco blog post (19 Oct. 2017), https://blogs.cisco.com/news/ciscos-200th-acquisition-a-tradition-of-advancement-disruption-and-growth (accessed 13 November 2018).
15 'Corporate Strategic Innovation Group', Cisco website, www.cisco.com/c/en/us/about/corporate-strategy-office/corporate-strategic-innovation-group.html (accessed 13 November 2018).
16 S. Kaplan, 'Zipcar Doesn't Just Ask Employees to Innovate – It Shows Them How', Harvard Business Review (1 Feb. 2017), https://hbr.org/2017/02/zipcar-doesnt-just-ask-employees-to-innovate-it-shows-them-how (accessed 11 November 2018).
17 For more detail on the rise of the sharing economy, see R. Botsman and R. Rogers, What's Mine is Yours: How Collaborative Consumption is Changing the Way We Live (London: Harper Collins, 2011).
18 P. Hobcraft, 'Understanding Innovation the WL Gore Way', Innovation Excellence (no date), www.innovationexcellence.com/blog/2011/09/28/understanding-innovation-the-w-l-gore-way (accessed 13 November 2018).
19 Á. Cain, 'The "two pizza rule" is Amazon CEO Jeff Bezos' secret to productive meetings', Business Insider UK (16 June 2017).
20 For more information on holocracy, see J. Morgan, 'The 5 Types Of Organizational Structures: Part 5, Holacratic Organizations', Forbes (20 July 2015) www.forbes.com/sites/jacobmorgan/2015/07/20/the-5-types-of-organizational-structures-part-5-holacratic-organizations (accessed 13 November 2018).
21 Z. Guzman, 'Zappos CEO Tony Hsieh on getting rid of managers: What I wish I'd done differently', CNBC Make It (13 Sept. 2016), www.cnbc.com/2016/09/13/zappos-ceo-tony-hsieh-the-thing-i-regret-about-getting-rid-of-managers.html (accessed 13 November 2018).

22   N. Statt, 'Zuckerberg: "Move fast and break things" isn't how Facebook operates anymore', *CNET* (30 Apr. 2014), www.cnet.com/news/zuckerberg-move-fast-and-break-things-isnt-how-we-operate-anymore (accessed 13 November 2018).

23   TechCrunch, 'Mark Zuckerberg Instructs Facebook to Move Fast' [video], YouTube (published 16 Sept. 2013), www.youtube.com/watch?v=V6urvN_4q9l.

24   'Dare to try' (no date), www.freibergs.com/resources/articles/innovation/dare-to-try (extracted from http://freibergs.com 11 November 2018).

25   R. Mukundan, S. Nandy, and R. Arora, '"Dare to Try": Culture Change at Tata Chemicals', *HQ Asia*, issue 3 (2012), p. 38, http://makinginnovationshappen.com/wp-content/uploads/2015/12/HQ-Asia-Issue-3-Dare-to-try.pdf (accessed 13 November 2018).

26   T. Soper, '"Failure and innovation are inseparable twins": Amazon founder Jeff Bezos offers 7 leadership principles', *GeekWire* (28 Oct. 2016), www.geekwire.com/2016/amazon-founder-jeff-bezos-offers-6-leadership-principles-change-mind-lot-embrace-failure-ditch-powerpoints (accessed 13 November 2018).

27   T. Lewis, 'Is Monzo the Facebook of banking?' *The Guardian* (17 Dec. 2017), www.theguardian.com/technology/2017/dec/17/monzo-facebook-of-banking (accessed 13 November 2018).

28   S. Vans-Colina, 'Save Spare Change with Coin Jar', Monzo blog post (7 Mar. 2018), https://monzo.com/blog/2018/03/07/coin-jar (accessed 13 November 2018).

29   J. Morgan, 'The Transformation of One of America's Most Iconic Companies' [podcast], (28 May 2017), https://thefutureorganization.com/transformation-one-americas-iconic-companies (accessed 13 November 2018).

30   C. Christensen, *The Innovator's Dilemma: When New Technologies Cause Great Companies to Fail*.

31   For a more in-depth analysis about the decline of Kodak, see S. D. Anthony, 'Kodak's Downfall Wasn't About Technology', *Harvard Business Review* (15 July 2016), https://hbr.org/2016/07/kodaks-downfall-wasnt-about-technology (accessed 13 November 2018).

32   C. M. Christensen and D. van Bever, 'The Capitalist's Dilemma', *Harvard Business Review* (June 2014), https://hbr.org/2014/06/the-capitalists-dilemma, (accessed 13 November 2018).

33   E. Ries, *The Lean Startup* (New York: Crown Publishing, 2011).

34   Frank Robinson actually coined the term 'minimal viable product': 'Minimal Viable Product', SyncDev website, www.syncdev.com/minimum-viable-product (accessed 13 November 2018).

35   See the Coca-Cola Company, Venturing and Emerging Brands website, www.vebatcoke.com.

36   C. Haley, J. Bone, and O. Allen, 'Incubators and accelerators: An updated directory for the UK', Nesta blog post (12 Apr. 2017), www.nesta.org.uk/blog/incubators-and-accelerators-an-updated-directory-for-the-uk (accessed 11 November 2018).

37   Y Combinator, www.ycombinator.com (accessed 11 November 2018).

38   Seedcamp, http://seedcamp.com (accessed 11 November 2018).

39   Rise, https://thinkrise.com (accessed 11 November 2018).

40   'NatWest sets up network of fintech accelerator hubs', *Finextra* (26 Feb. 2018), www.finextra.com/newsarticle/31733/natwest-sets-up-network-of-fintech-accelerator-hubs (accessed 11 November 2018).

41   Fidelity Labs, www.fidelitylabs.com (accessed 11 November 2018).

42   C. Haley, S. Bielli, and V. Mocker, 'Winning Together: A guide to successful corporate-startup collaborations', Nesta report (16 June 2015), www.nesta.org.uk/report/winning-together-a-guide-to-successful-corporate-startup-collaborations (accessed 11 November 2018).

43   C. M. Christensen, *Competing Against Luck* (New York: HarperBusiness, 2016).

44   C. M. Christensen, T. Hall, K. Dillon, and D. S. Duncan, 'Know Your Customers' "Jobs to Be Done"', *Harvard Business Review* (Sept. 2016), https://hbr.org/2016/09/know-your-customers-jobs-to-be-done (accessed 11 November 2018).

45   C. Christensen, 'The "Job" of a McDonald's Milkshake' [video], YouTube (published 5 Oct. 2017), www.youtube.com/watch?v=QEFAHIulWw4 (accessed 11 November 2018).

46   C. M. Christensen et al, 'Know Your Customers' "Jobs to be Done"'.

47   R. G. McGrath, 'The customer rarely buys what the company thinks it's selling him: "Understanding the jobs" theory', www.linkedin.com/pulse/understanding-jobs-theory-rita-gunther-mcgrath (accessed 13 November 2018).

48   C. Salter, 'Marissa Mayer's 9 Principles of Innovation', *Fast Company* (19 Feb. 2008), www.fastcompany.com/702926/marissa-mayers-9-principles-innovation (accessed 11 November 2018).

49   As measured by the organisation's employee opinion survey and attrition rates.

50   J. L. Heskett, T. O. Jones, G. W. Loveman, W. E. Sasser, Jr., and L. A. Schlesinger, 'Putting the Service-Profit Chain to Work', *Harvard Business Review* (July–Aug. 2008), https://hbr.org/2008/07/putting-the-service-profit-chain-to-work (accessed 13 November 2018).

51   D. Pink, *Drive: The Surprising Truth about What Motivates Us*, (Edinburgh: Canongate Books, 2009).

52   S. Glucksberg, 'The influence of strength of drive on functional fixedness and perceptual recognition', *Journal of Experimental Psychology*, vol. 63, no. 1 (1962), pp. 36–41.

53   D. Pink, 'The puzzle of motivation' [video], TEDGlobal (July 2009), www.ted.com/talks/dan_pink_on_motivation (accessed 13 November 2018).

54   N. Bennett and G. J. Lemoine, 'What VUCA Really Means for You', *Harvard Business Review* (Jan.–Feb. 2014), https://hbr.org/2014/01/what-vuca-really-means-for-you (accessed 11 November 2018).

55   D. Pink, 'The puzzle of motivation' [video], TED Summaries (posted 6 June 2014), https://tedsummaries.com/2014/06/06/dan-pink-the-puzzle-of-motivation (accessed 11 November 2018).

56   For more information on the demise of Encarta see N. Cohen, 'Microsoft Encarta Dies After Long Battle With Wikipedia', *Bits* (30 Mar. 2009), https://bits.blogs.nytimes.com/2009/03/30/microsoft-encarta-dies-after-long-battle-with-wikipedia (accessed 11 November 2018).

57   D. Pink, *Drive: The Surprising Truth about What Motivates Us*, p. 203.

58   For more detail on Braintrust at Pixar, see E. Catmull, 'Inside The Pixar Braintrust', *Fast Company* (12 Mar. 2014), www.fastcompany.com/3027135/inside-the-pixar-braintrust.

59   Front End of Innovation Conference 2017, Seaport World Trade Center, Boston, 8–11 May 2017, E. Catmull, keynote address.

60   E. Catmull keynote address, Front End of Innovation Conference 2017.

61   E. Catmull keynote address, Front End of Innovation Conference 2017.

62   E. Catmull, 'Inside The Pixar Braintrust'.

63   JLABS, 'JPALing around with Stef Dhanda', JLABS blog post (18 Oct. 2017), https://jlabs.jnjinnovation.com/blog/jpaling-around-stef-dhanda (accessed 11 November 2018).

64   'Kickbox, Level 2: Step 4', Adobe Kickbox website, https://kickbox.adobe.com/workshop/kickbox/7d625387/section2/step4 (accessed 11 November 2018).

65   M. Wilson, 'Adobe's Kickbox: The Kit To Launch Your Next Big Idea', *Fast Company* (9 Feb. 2015), www.fastcompany.com/3042128/adobes-kickbox-the-kit-to-launch-your-next-big-idea (accessed 11 November 2018).

66   H. Lippe, 'Design Thinking… what's that?' Fidelity Labs blog post (5 Jan. 2017), www.fidelitylabs.com/2017/01/05/design-thinkingwhats-that (accessed 11 November 2018).

67   A. Goryachev, 'Igniting a Companywide Startup Culture of Entrepreneurs', Cisco blog post (9 June 2016), https://blogs.cisco.com/innovation/igniting-a-companywide-startup-culture-of-entrepreneurs (accessed 11 November 2018).

68   See Chapter Two.

Acknowledgements

Firstly, I would like to thank Joe Nagle for his support and advice throughout the writing of this book. He read many drafts, always gave great advice, and was invaluable with the final operations for getting it to print.

I owe a huge debt to the real-world innovators who very kindly shared their experiences with me. Particularly, thank you to Harvey Wade, Nic Roome, Magdalena Krön and Will Reddaway.

This book would never have happened without the inspiration and advice of Daniel Priestley and Lucy McCarraher. Also, thanks must go out to my fantastic coach Alison Warner, who has always been there with words of advice, encouragement and the occasional bold challenge.

The team at The Innovation Beehive works ceaselessly with our clients to help build their Innovation Ecosystems. Your stories and experiences have been invaluable to me whilst writing this book.

Thank you to the wonderful Jen Alexander and Anna-Louise Walters at Google, who have been so supportive of The Innovation Beehive and who hosted many wonderful Innovation Ecosystem events for our clients.

Our friends at Airbnb very kindly supported the launch of The Innovation Ecosystem when it was still a White Paper in 2017. Thank you to Nic Roome and Kate Walsh for living your brand so beautifully and hosting us so well.

And finally, thank you to The Innovation Beehive's clients. For inviting us into your businesses, and for going on the journey with us.

The Author

Mok O'Keeffe has over two decades' experience of working in innovation in Europe, the United States, the Middle East and Asia. He has worked alongside, studied and visited some of the world's most innovative organisations and seen first hand how they build an Innovation Ecosystem. Mok is the Founder of The Innovation Beehive, whose clients include Google, McDonald's Corporation, Ford Motor Company, Hearst Magazines and Lloyds Banking Group. He has been quoted in *Forbes Magazine*, *People Manager* and *HR Magazine*, and is a regular keynote speaker on innovation, culture and leadership.